W9-BUM-232

The Mystery of Marriage

20th anniversary edition

the
mystery
of
marriage

meditations on
the miracle

mike mason

Multnomah® Publishers *Sisters, Oregon*

THE MYSTERY OF MARRIAGE
published by Multnomah Publishers, Inc.

Published in association with the literary agency of Alive Communications, Inc., 7680
Goddard Street, Suite 200, Colorado Springs, CO 80920
© 1985, 2005 by Mike Mason
International Standard Book Number: 1-59052-374-1 (pb)
Special CBD version: 1-59052-571-X (hb)

Scripture quotations have been adapted by the author from *The Holy Bible,*
New International Version © 1973, 1984 by International Bible Society,
used by permission of Zondervan Publishing House.

Multnomah is a trademark of Multnomah Publishers, Inc.,
and is registered in the U.S. Patent and Trademark Office.
The colophon is a trademark of Multnomah Publishers, Inc.

Printed in the United States of America
First printing of 20th Anniversary Edition 2005

ALL RIGHTS RESERVED
No part of this publication may be reproduced, stored in a retrieval system, or
transmitted, in any form or by any means—electronic, mechanical, photocopying,
recording, or otherwise—without prior written permission.

For information:
MULTNOMAH PUBLISHERS, INC.
POST OFFICE BOX 1720
SISTERS, OREGON 97759

05 06 07 08 09 10 11 12—31 30 29 28 27 26 25

OVERTON MEMORIAL LIBRARY
HERITAGE CHRISTIAN UNIVERSITY
P.O. Box HCU
Florence, Alabama 35630

For (who else?) Karen

"Many women do noble things,

but you surpass them all."

— PROVERBS 31:29

Contents

Foreword

If any recently married student of mine at Regent College who wanted to be a writer had consulted me about making marriage the theme of his first book, I should have told him as pontifically as I could that however natural the thought in light of his own present condition, it was a no-no, and he must put it out of his mind. I should have explained that marriage, being the most delicate and demanding of human relationships, as well as potentially the most delightful, is a terribly difficult topic on which to write wisely and well. I should have pointed out that the Christian world is already full of bad books on marriage, books written, it seems, by extrovert Pharisees for readers like themselves who want to reduce life to routines of role-play, and that he could hardly hope to escape the influence of these well-meant but dreadful models. I should have observed that it takes married folk years and years to get their togetherness into perspective, and that young authors rarely write with any depth about relationships anyway. And so on, and so forth. I should have discouraged him every way I could and been sure that thereby I was doing him a service.

Fortunately for the world, and for me as well, as it now turns out, Mike Mason, having sat thoughtfully through some classes of mine, did not consult me about what he planned to do, but went right ahead and did it, with the result that is now before you—this outstanding achievement, of which I would have deprived you if Mike had asked and taken my advice. For better, for worse (I may appropriately borrow that phrase, I think), I write a lot of forewords these days: Packer's *nihil obstat* is prized by some. Rarely, however, has a new book roused in me so much enthusiasm as has the combination of wisdom, depth, dignity, and *glow*—I don't know what else to call it—that I find in these chapters. To introduce them is not a chore but an excitement.

Christians, read them—but slowly! Their tone quality, resonating as it does off the Bible as its sounding board, is richer than we are used to. Couples, read them together! Your awe and joy at what you have got into will be mightily fed. Multnomah Publishers, commission some more books from Mike Mason!—for this one is a crackerjack. And readers, please excuse my own slight giddiness; Mike's pages have just made me aware again that I too am a man in love. For the freshness and force with which he spells out the magnificence of marriage in God's plan I am deeply grateful, and I predict that the same will soon be true of many more.

James Packer

❦ *Preface* ❦

There are many ways of measuring the success of a book. I measure the success of this one by the friends it has given me.

From the beginning it is a book that has made friends. One of my favorites is Laurie Hills of Manistee, Michigan. About a year after *The Mystery of Marriage* appeared, she wrote to say that she was driving around the country teaching at various seminars, and wherever she went she kept a box of my books in her car and was handing them out left and right. By that point my book had received some fine reviews, and my publisher was most enthusiastic. But the day I heard from Laurie Hills, I knew I had written a good book.

Over the years many other friends have written letters, or phoned, or appeared in the most unexpected settings to tell me how much this book has meant to them. Many people have read it two or three times, many have bought one copy and given away six. Most heartwarming of all are those countless couples who tell me they have read the book aloud to each other. This still amazes and delights me whenever I hear it. It's one thing for parents to read aloud to children. But when adults take time to read aloud to each other, it seems to me some fantastic good must be afoot in the world. I'll bet the angels gather to listen, and I think the earth must shift a little on its axis.

People like those mentioned above have taught me that, as I write the words of this new preface, I'm not writing to a blank page, but to a great gathered company of my friends. This thought is like a warm fire that illumines the four walls of my study. It has brought tremendous life to my writing. For friends, when all is said and done, are what a writer wants. Writing can be a lonely life. Certainly it is a solitary one, or has been for me. It's not just the writing itself that must be done all alone in a room; it means a relatively solitary lifestyle too. I don't know any way of writing well without spending a good deal of time reading, thinking, and praying. Especially praying. In fact the recipe for me has always been about three hours of prayer for every hour of writing. That's a lot of time spent alone in the closet!

How I thank God, then, that from the start He has given me a loving wife to be my best friend of all. She is (as the poem at the end of the book suggests) my monastery. For having set out in the Christian life to become a monk, I found myself instead falling in love with a woman. At first I worried intensely that I'd made a huge mistake, fallen prey to a terrible temptation. But what a surprise it was to discover, over the years, that as a married man (and a father too) I have become more and more a true monk than I ever could have been within the walls of a monastery. How is this? It's because love, true love, sets people free to be whoever they are.

Many times I have told Karen that she is the best wife in the world, and I really believe it. Also that she is the most beautiful and wonderful of all women, and I believe that too. She is like Eve to me, the only woman on earth. Of course she is a sinner as I am. But when, like God, we choose to look past this in each other, we enter the paradise of love.

When I wrote *The Mystery of Marriage,* I was entering into paradise, and knew it. It was the second year of our marriage; we'd worked out a few of the kinks. We were living in a beautiful summer house among the mountains in Hope, British Columbia. It was winter, and the uninsulated house was cold. We slept beneath piles of blankets, and in my study I had no less than three heaters: a propane room heater, a portable electric, and a heating pad for my feet. As I typed, I looked out on a view of mountains and the rushing Coquihalla River. Except for right now, I have never been happier in my life.

What I did that winter was to take the journals I had kept during the period of our engagement and turn them into a book on marriage. It was pretty simple. The real writing had already been done; I was just editing. Many people are surprised at this, surprised that the material for an insightful marriage book was mainly composed prior to marriage. But it's true. During that rhapsodic, tumultuous year of betrothal I wrote down everything, all the thoughts that were coming to me about love, both the pains and the joys. If there's anything of truth in this book, it's because the writer was (and is) head over heels in love. For the wisest of all people is the one who's in love, isn't that right?

But there's another secret to this book, which is that during that year of premarriage I also happened to be a new Christian. In fact, I was writing about my love affair with Jesus. I was writing my prayer life. My love for God got all mixed up with my love for Karen. It began to seem all the same to me, which indeed it is. Love is love. If we truly have the love of God, we will find that it spills over to everyone around us. First to those closest to us, then out and out like ripples in a pond. We will find that marriage is a perfect metaphor for the love of God, and that the same is true of parenting, friendship, the church, nature, or anything else in life.

This is the way God planned it, that everything in our lives should perfectly reflect His love, so that His glory covers the earth. Everything we experience is a door into paradise.

The only trouble is, many of us are going through the door the wrong way, exiting instead of entering. These are tough times for marriage. Statistics on divorce, to say nothing of abuses within marriage, are higher than ever. But I feel the opposite is also true. As the kingdom of darkness advances, the kingdom of light advances even more. More than ever before in history, couples who submit wholeheartedly in marriage, both to God and to one another, stand on the threshold of paradise, of pure bliss. I believe this is a gift of God available right now to anyone who wants it— not only in marriages but in all relationships.

Why not, today, reach out one hand to the Lord, and the other to your mate, and step into the Garden?

Mike Mason

an aerial parable

Prologue

There are three things that are too

amazing for me,

four that I do not understand:

the way of an eagle in the sky,

the way of a snake on a rock,

the way of a ship on the high seas,

and the way of a man with a maiden."

—Proverbs 30:18 19

Prologue

The week of our honeymoon, my wife and I stopped one after-
noon at a Trappist monastery. It was a hot summer day, the air
bright and still, and the sky a deep, dusty blue. Nothing moved.
There wasn't a monk in sight. We got out of our car and strolled
hand in hand toward the monastery, and soon we emerged from
the hot blue brightness of the day into the cool silent chapel, where
there was a brightness of a different kind, and an interior stillness
too, that was quite different from the stillness outside. Our hands
fell apart, and a feeling of awkwardness crept over me, an embarrassment. I suppose I was wondering what God really thought of
this marriage of mine.

We knelt to pray. The stillness clamored, echoed all over the
building like shouts. It was reflecting my heart, echoing back to
me my own confusion. All the questions and doubts from the time
of our engagement came rushing back. What was it all about, this
marriage? And was it for real now? How could I have gone through
with it? Was it really too late to back out? Who was this woman
anyway? Couldn't I just stay here and become a monk? The silence
of the chapel beat like wings all around us but offered not one particle of consolation.

On the way out we met the guestmaster, a man who knew me.

I introduced my new wife to him and felt ashamed. Certainly it would be all too clear to him, I thought, what a terrible mistake I had made. We exchanged pleasantries, then turned to go, and as we drove out the long, treed lane that leads away from that beautiful place, I felt about as hopelessly trapped and as irredeemably desolate as I have ever felt in my life.

At the end of the lane we came to the main road, where the trees stopped and fields of ripe, blond wheat opened out in front of us and stretched away to meet the blue distance. And now another kind of stillness had descended upon us; not the stillness of this great shining day nor the stillness of the little chapel, but a new stillness, an eerie and agonizing stillness between my wife and me, the loudest stillness of all.

Suddenly she pointed to a tiny dark dot above the wheat, far away, but moving, coming this way. We watched, and soon realized that there was a second dot as well, and that the two dots were circling around each other. Occasionally they appeared to intersect, only to come apart again.

"Hawks," said my wife.

"Yes, hawks," I said.

The pair were still very high up, but as they drew closer to us, they began to descend in great lazy swoops down the blue invisible banisters of the air. It looked as if they were coming down especially for the purpose of putting on a show for us. I parked the car, and we got out to watch. They were quite plain now. The sunlight spilled soft auras around their splayed forms. We could see frayed feathers, translucent at the tips. Not once did either bird move a wing muscle. They held themselves perfectly steady, taut yet relaxed, angling against the air and gliding as if they were a part of it, just two molecules of the empty air made visible, turning in slow and beautiful spirals that meshed together and then away like gears, like a pair of ice skaters. One turned clockwise and the other counter, and gyring down and down they seemed to form the vortex of the day's stillness.

The longer we watched the clearer it became that these hawks were doing absolutely nothing of any practical import: They were not hunting, for example, or looking for anything, or going anywhere. They were simply playing. They were enjoying the warm blueness of the day, the strength and skill in their wings, the fun of flying, and (perhaps most of all) the fun of each other. I do not know much about hawks, but what struck me at the time, curiously, was that I could not recall having ever seen two hawks together. Whenever I had seen a hawk before, I thought, hadn't it always been alone? So there was something in this soaring dance of the pair of them, with a whole sky all to themselves, that spoke directly to me, not just of play and freedom on a summer's day, but of the shining beauty of love, the pure ease and joy of companionship.

We watched this stunning aerial parable for a long time, my wife and I, and when eventually the great birds turned again into tiny dots in the golden blue distance and we climbed back into our car, there was yet another kind of stillness that descended upon us: the stillness of perfect understanding.

This book grew out of that experience of the two hawks playing in the wide-open summer sky outside the Trappist monastery on our honeymoon. It grew, in other words, out of a deeply rooted conflict in myself, the conflict between a yearning for solitude and a yearning for companionship, and out of the beginnings of the resolution of that conflict. It grew out of the slow and gentle demolishing of a misconception I had had about the married life, and I suppose about life and love in general: For I had never seen the great blue sky of freedom against which marriage, and indeed all relationships, are played out. As a single Christian I had come to think of myself, rather pompously, as being celibate, when the truth of the matter was that I was just a hard-bitten bachelor, who had never considered that in getting married one espouses not an institution but a person, not a narrowness but an unimaginable breadth of possibility. For a person is the single most limitless entity in creation, and if there is anything that is even more unlimited and unrestrained in its possibilities than is a person, it is two people together.

Not everyone is as fond of solitude as I have been. And certainly not everyone has seriously entertained the notion of entering the cloister, only to find himself falling in love and getting married instead. But that is how marriage came to me. And marriage comes to everyone, I think, with something of the same surprise, the same reversal of fortunes, the same searching exposure of deep-seated conflict. Not only that, but whatever a person's temperament or circumstances might be, it seems to me that the conflict which marriage uncovers is always essentially this same one: It is always some version of this tension between the needs for dependence and for independence, between the urge toward loving cooperation and the opposite urge toward detachment, privacy, self-sufficiency. Even to people who have dreamed for years about getting married and who think of themselves as hating to be alone, marriage still cannot help but come as an invasion of privacy. No one has ever been married without being surprised, and usually alarmed, at the sheer intensity of this invasion.

So I was alarmed. From the moment I met my wife, I sensed that a process of interior disintegration was beginning to work in me, systematically, insidiously. In other ways, of course, I was being rejuvenated, tremendously built up. But a thirty-year-old man is like a densely populated city: Nothing new can be built, in its heart, without something else being torn down. So I began to be demolished. There were many times when I felt quite seriously that everything my life had stood for was being challenged, or that somehow I had been tricked into selling my very soul for the sake of a woman's love! So there was a lot at stake as the wedding day approached: In fact, there was everything at stake. Never before had I felt that so much was riding upon one single decision. Later I would discover, very gradually, that that is one of the chief characteristics of love: It asks for everything. Not just for a little bit, or a whole lot, but for everything. And unless one is challenged to give everything, one is not really in love.

But how hard it is to give everything! Indeed, it is impossible. One can make a symbolic gesture of giving all, accompanied by a grand dramatic public statement to that effect (which is what happens at the wedding ceremony). But that is just a start. The wedding is merely the beginning of a lifelong process of handing over absolutely everything, and not simply everything that one owns but everything that one is.

There is no one who is not broken by this process. It is excruciating and inexorable, and no one can stand up to it. Everyone gets broken on the wheel of love, and the breaking that takes place is like nothing else under the sun. It is not like the breaking that happens in bankruptcy or in a crop failure or in the loss of a job or the collapse of a lifetime's work. It is not even like the breaking that takes place in a body wracked by a painful disease. For in marriage the breaking that is done is done by the very heel of love itself. It is not physical pain or natural disaster or the terrible evil world that is to blame, but rather it is love, love itself that breaks us. And that is the hardest thing of all to take. For in the wrestling ring of this life, it is love that is our solar plexus. That is where things really hurt. There is no hurt like the hurt that happens in the place where we love. And when anything at all goes wrong in a marriage, that is the place to be affected. That is the vulnerable place in all human relationships. What is on the line, always, with every person we meet, is our capacity to love and to be loved. But whereas in most other relationships our vulnerability in this respect can be hidden, more or less (and how expert we are at hiding it!), in the relationship of marriage it is this very quality of vulnerability that is exposed, exalted, exploited. And this is the thing that can prove to be too much for people, too much to handle. Many give up and run away, their entire lives collapsing in ruins. But even those who hang on face inevitable ruin, for they must be broken too.

There is an important difference, however, between those who hang on and those who run away, between the marriages that last and are good, and the ones that either break up or else drag on in a state of unresolved tension and neurosis. Both must endure ruin, but the difference lies in the *place* in which this ruin is experienced. For in those who run away from the intense fire of marriage, the ruin happens in the place in them that is love, and this place, this glorious and mysterious and delicate capacity in them, really does receive a terrible wound, sometimes enough to impair it for life. But in the case of those who hang on to love and who see it through to its mortal finish, the ruin that occurs, the internal debacle, is not in the place of love (although it may often seem to be happening there), but rather in the place, in the palace, of the ego. And that makes all the difference in the world. It is one thing to wreck the ego. But it is quite another, and indeed the very opposite, to make shipwreck of the soul.

One of the hardest things in marriage is the feeling of being watched. It is the constant surveillance that can get to one, that can wear one down like a bright light shining in the eyes, and that leads inevitably to the crumbling of all defenses, all facades, all the customary shams and masquerades of the personality. Does this make marriage sound like some ordeal of brainwashing? But actually that is very much the sort of effect it has, with the single exception that the one doing the brainwashing, the one holding the bright light, is not some ruthless prosecutor or torturer, but love. It is love that pins us to the wall and makes us answer, and makes us keep on answering until the answer that comes out is the one that love wants to hear.

So it can be hard to be watched, to have one's whole life put under surveillance, and for the person who does not want to be spied upon, it makes scant difference whether the watcher be love or something more sinister. What is hard is the watchfulness. For we are opaque, solid creatures; we resist being transparent. And yet that is what love asks for: transparency.

Matrimony, then, through this devastating strategy of watching, launches a fierce and unrelenting attack upon the fortress of the ego, upon that place in a person that craves privacy, independence, self-sufficiency, lack of interference. Nevertheless, for the couple able to withstand this assault and who mature together in love, there is a great surprise in store, for there is a gradual discovery that marriage at its best possesses an uncanny power for deeply gratifying this very ego, this peculiar separateness of each person, even as it chastens it. Marriage, in other words, turns out to be the best of two worlds, satisfying all of the needs relating to separateness and solitude, together with those of companionship. Think what it is like, for example, to be alone with one's beloved, to be silent and still and enthralled, with no other purpose than that of being together, being alone with love. It is, oddly enough, an experience of being neither alone nor not-alone, but rather about midway between the two, and somehow involving the very best of both experiences. It means that one can totally relax, but with a relaxation that nevertheless has an edge to it, for there is always the awareness that one is being watched. And yet, being watched by one who loves is not like being watched by anyone else on earth! No, to be loved as one is being watched is like one thing only: It is like the watchfulness of the Lord God Himself, the sense that the believer has of living out his life in the invisible presence of the living God, and of being so loved that it is as if an aura or halo had already been conferred upon him, a spiritual electricity that surrounds and fills all of his words and actions, for suddenly all that he is and does is not only accepted and respected, but marveled at. More than just being appreciated, he is treated as being awesome, beautiful. He is cherished.

Under such treatment, of course, a person is given the opportunity of opening like a flower and becoming perfectly natural, perfectly himself. And yet this true self of his turns out, surprisingly, to be someone he himself has never met before, someone just mysteriously different enough from the real self he thought he was that it can only be described, finally, as someone entirely new. Or someone who has been there all along, perhaps, but who has finally become self-confident enough, through the grace of love, to step out of the shadows. For that is what love does: It brings people out into the light, no matter how painful that transition might prove to be. Love aims at revelation, at a clarifying and defining of our true natures. It is a sort of sharpening process, a paring away of dull and lifeless exteriors so that the keen new edge of a person's true self can begin to flash and gleam in the light of day.

A diamond cannot be cut with a tin saw, and neither can a hawk fly with a butterfly. A person, to grow keen and shining and real, needs love, which is to say, needs another person: "As iron sharpens iron, so one person sharpens another" (Proverbs 27:17). And sharpening is a painful process: Extract the pain from love, and there is nothing left.

When I saw those two hawks, therefore, I took them as a sign, as a sign of God's pleasure in my marriage, and as His promise that above and beyond the hurt, the uncertainty, the growing pains of the sharpening process, showers of crystal fiery sparks were flying up into the blue roof of heaven. It was not just hawks that were flying, but angels that were dancing on account of my marriage, and any yearning I might have had to be in a monastery (besides being ludicrously unrealistic by that point) was nothing less than a temptation from the devil. Those two hawks were a confirmation that, for me at least, no worship could be more pleasing or acceptable to God than the worship of marital love, of two lives being played out against one another in a covenant of loving cooperation. What happened to me that summer's day was one of those gentle eruptions of grace that the Lord sends so quietly, so nonchalantly, so playfully into our lives, but which has the power to explode our inhumanities in our faces and to set within us a clean, new heart. Never again would I have excuse to give in to those crippling and agonizing doubts as to whether God had called me to be married, or whether He had called me to be married to this particular woman.

And never again could I think of marriage as in any sense separate from or subordinate to the life of faith. Indeed, if it is true that a Christian cannot think about God without simultaneously think-ing of Jesus Christ, then it is equally true that a Christian husband comes to think more and more of his wife in relation to Christ and his promise to follow Him. That is how closely a man's marriage is bound up with his love for God. "Husbands," instructs Paul, "love your wives, just as Christ loved the church" (Ephesians 5:25). Marriage for the Christian is a continuous sacrament, an act of praise and obedience, and a means of grace that is inherently every bit as spiritual as anything that goes on in a monastery, or in any church or mission field for that matter, and every bit as important (or more) as any other work that one might do in the world. For the entertaining of a sanctimonious longing for the cloister is not the only way to try to worm out of one's marriage vows! My feel-ings in the Trappist chapel were just one glaring instance of the central temptation that, often in far more subtle ways, haunts every marriage: the lack of wholehearted commitment. There is a secret resentment of the demands of marriage, a reluctance to give away any more than is absolutely necessary. There is a constant tempta-tion to pull back from the full intensity of the relationship, to get along on only the basic requirements. But set against this is the con-stant challenge to give more and more of oneself, at deeper and deeper levels, and to see in one's partner a most abundant and per-fect channel for the outpouring of the grace of God into one's life.

A long time after the incident of the two hawks, my wife and I were standing on a mountain overlooking the Pacific Ocean, and we saw another sight that neither of us had ever seen before. This time it was a pair of eagles, doing just what the hawks had done: circling around and around one another, lazily but with exquisite concentration, wings held perfectly steady, bodies cruciform with flight. And this time we looked not up at these beautiful birds, but down upon their backs, for we ourselves stood upon a higher place. It was New Year's Day, and behind us lay a year of not inconsiderable struggle. But now, once more, the sky was cloudless and the air dancing with sun as the Lord opened His hands and released these two golden birds as one more sign to us of His enormous pleasure in our married love. The eagles were a good thousand feet below us, and twice that distance below them lay the blue, blue water of the Pacific, catching all the sun's gold and carrying it wave upon sparkling wave right off the end of the world. The air was so clear that day that we were able to see, perhaps, farther than we ever have in our lives.

God never sends just one sign: He keeps on confirming His course for us with one vision after another. But the reading of His signs is essentially a task for faith, a task for people who are willing to persist in seeking out the correspondence between the external and visible realities of their lives, and the interior weather of their souls, striving always to bring the two into line in order that the kingdom of God might come. For the interior journey is necessarily an exterior journey, the path to God necessarily the path of deepening human relationships. Marriage stands at the very hub of this exciting spiritual dialectic, for it is, as Paul points out, a cameo dramatization of the relationship of the whole church with its Lord and Savior Jesus Christ.

This is the territory this book seeks to explore, this dynamic correspondence between marriage and the great invisible realities of the Christian faith. It is not a "how-to" book so much as a "how-come" book, a meditative inquiry into the spiritual foundations upon which marriage is built.

ONE

we are not alone

Otherness

As iron sharpens iron,

so one person sharpens another.

— PROVERBS 27:17

Otherness

THE FIRST MIRACLE

When I first proposed to a friend the initial four words of a verse from Proverbs—"as iron sharpens iron"—as the basis for a book on marriage, he wanted to know what I planned to say about the verses that immediately precede it: "A quarrelsome wife is like a constant dripping on a rainy day; restraining her is like restraining the wind or grasping oil with the hand" (Proverbs 27:15–16).

The Bible is such a tactless book, isn't it? So coarse in places, so unkind and indelicate, so deeply unromantic. But surely marriage is also a tactless affair, full of awkwardness and indelicacy, as unromantic at times as a sink full of dirty dishes. Whether one's mate happens to be a quarrelsome creature or not, marriage still has an uncanny knack for creating a more or less "constant dripping" in one's life. It is not all smooth sailing in a cloudless sky! Nevertheless, a beleaguered spouse will do well to bear in mind an observation of Jeremy Taylor's: "a husband must learn to tolerate his wife's infirmities, because in doing so he either cures her, or makes himself better." (These remarks, needless to say, must apply equally to husbands as to wives!)

Despite the caustic comments about shrewish wives sprinkled throughout Proverbs, it is with a sustained paean to marital bliss that the book ends:

> *A wife of noble character who can find?*
> *She is worth far more than rubies.*
> *Her husband has full confidence in her*
> *and lacks nothing of value.*
>
> PROVERBS 31:10–11

In other words, the book of Proverbs as a whole takes a view of marriage that remains proverbial to this day: There is nothing in the world worse than a bad marriage, and at the same time nothing better than a good one.

And that, in some ways, is the whole message of biblical theology, for throughout the Bible marriage is employed as the most sublime metaphor for the relationship between man and God. Paul, as we have noted, resorted to this picture to describe the loving union between Christ and His Church, but the Old Testament prophets also used marriage as the plainest and most transparent example of the type of covenant love the Lord has for His people, and Jesus told parables in which a wedding feast became the symbolic setting for the coming of the kingdom. A good Christian marriage, indeed, is more than a religious metaphor: It is a first, tangible, visible, and most glorious fruit of the kingdom of God. A wedding was the occasion not only for the first miracle of Jesus; it was, after Creation itself, God's own first miracle: "He brought the woman to the man" (Genesis 2:22).

Surely no encounter between two people, anywhere in history or in literature, is more famous than the meeting between Adam and Eve in Paradise. When Stanley came upon Livingstone in the heart of Africa, he found only what he had been looking for. But what if he had not been looking? What if neither of them had ever seen another white man? What if neither of them had ever seen another human being? Or perhaps we may be reminded of Defoe's Robinson Crusoe, stooping down to examine footprints not his own on the beach of his lonely island. But what might have been his astonishment if, cast away not from any shipwreck but fresh from the hand of his Creator, he had supposed himself to be the only person on earth? Or what if Friday had turned out to be a woman rather than a man, and if Crusoe had never even dreamed of the possibility of there being a female of his species?

Fantastic as such conjectures may sound, they are all elements that are electrically present in the dramatic Genesis account of the original meeting between man and woman, the meeting of the first two human beings. We can only dimly imagine the sort of thoughts that must have raced through Adam's brain on that occasion, but we do have a record of what he said, and what he said was, simply, "This is now bone of my bones and flesh of my flesh; she shall be called 'woman,' for she was taken out of man" (Genesis 2:23). Was Adam more interested in etymology than in love, and more fascinated with osteology than he was with sex? His comment is, interestingly, the first true poetry in the Bible, yet it may strike our modern ears as being decidedly prosaic.

It must be remembered, however, that this odd remark comes only after Adam had surveyed and named every other creature in the world and found not one that he could really identify with, let alone one that would be a suitable friend or partner for him. But at the sight of Eve his heart leaped with recognition. Here was a creature who was as close as possible to being like himself and yet was different. She was different in two respects, in fact, for not only was she a distinct and separate person, but she was differently made. Even the manner of her formation had been distinctive: not out of the dust but out of Adam's own side. And so, in spite of the difference and in spite of the apartness, the man intuitively recognized that here was a creature who, unlike anything else he had yet laid eyes on, somehow fell into the same unique category of creation that he himself did, and was therefore his equal. More than an alter ego, she was a sort of alter id. Something deeper in Adam than he knew how to articulate responded to her, finding a home in her, and a sense of family. She was bone of his bone, and he saw that she was covered with his own flesh. She was his own flesh and blood.

And this, the Genesis account goes on to tell us, is the reason for marriage: "This is why a man leaves his father and mother and joins himself to his wife, and they become one flesh" (Genesis 2:24). Why? It is because of this mysterious, compelling combination of identity and otherness. After we have surveyed, as far as possible, all the other creatures in the world, eventually God presents us with one who is special, one who strikes a deeper chord in us than anyone else was able to do. Although the person may be very unlike us in many important ways, still there is something inside us that recognizes the other as being bone of our bone and flesh of our flesh, akin to us on a level far deeper than personality. This is a blood tie, an affinity of the heart in every sense. It is as if we discover an actual kinship with the one we love, which the marriage ceremony serves only to make official. To be married is to have found in a total stranger a near and long-lost relative, a true blood relative even closer to us than father or mother.

The Original Encounter

We may presume that we cannot know, as Adam did, what it is like to see another human being for the very first time, let alone a person of the opposite sex. Yet in a sense we can, for it is something of this very same primal and unimaginable wonderment that has been preserved and enshrined for us, even today, in the simple and lowly state of holy matrimony. In marriage a man is given the opportunity of seeing one woman, one person, as he has never seen any other woman or person before. Marriage not only affords as deep a glimpse into the heart and soul of another being as we shall ever have, but it cannot survive without deliberately striving to preserve the spontaneity and freshness of this insight. And how we long for such freshness! There is a giddy taste of it in the experience of falling in love, but only a loving marriage provides the long, deep, steady draught of it that, perhaps without even knowing it, we crave. For secretly we long to perpetuate that one astounding moment in the Garden of Eden. We long to stand in awe of one another, just as Adam and Eve must have done when they first locked gazes. We long for our whole body to tingle with the thrill of knowing that this one fascinating being, this being of a different gender, has been created especially for us and given to us unreservedly for our help, comfort, and joy. Men and women ache for the heart with which to know this reality, and for the eyes with which to see one another (and therefore themselves) as the astounding miracles that they are.

This is what marriage is about. This is the one central experience it seeks to capture, to explore, and to exploit to the fullest. The encounter between the first man and the first woman is the archetypal stuff out of which marriage has been built. Marriage is made of this encounter as the body is made of flesh, and it is the work of marriage continually to return to this encounter, to recapture it afresh and to feed upon it. Most marriages are invaded sooner or later by the suspicion that the partners may really have very little in common beyond the simple fact that they are both human beings and that they happen to love each other (or at least thought they did at one time). It can be a very great shock for a couple to discover how quickly romantic love is exhausted, how little they really know or understand one another, how deeply estranged it is possible to become from the person you thought you were closest to. Even a taste of such estrangement can be enough to fill a couple with fear and to plunge them into permanent grief over having made such a "poor choice" of partner: Why couldn't they have chosen someone with whom they had more natural affinity?

And yet it is this fundamental *apartness,* this same sense of nothing else in common but human flesh itself and the primal attraction between man and woman, that is the very strength of a marriage, and the experience to which the relationship must constantly return for nourishment. For it is right here that the mystery of love can best be discerned and known. This is the soil in which love thrives, a rich, black, mysterious loam of total darkness in which nothing else will grow. How else can true love be truly known except when it is separated from everything that is like it, from all forms of natural attraction? A marriage lives, paradoxically, upon those almost impossible times when it is perfectly clear to the two partners that nothing else but pure sacrificial love can hold them together.

Of course, it is almost always the case that the couple has much more in common than they may suppose. But marriage seems to specialize, at times, in radically de-emphasizing the similarities between the partners and wildly exaggerating the points of difference (especially at the superficial level of personality or temperament). But this is so that a couple may come to know one another at the deepest level, at the only level that really matters: bone of bone, flesh of flesh. It is so that the wondrous surprise of the original encounter in the Garden of Eden may take place all over again. It is so that a couple may be reduced to sheer amazement that they are together at all, and that they may know that what has brought them together and what keeps them together is something entirely outside of themselves, something not natural but supernatural, something they themselves cannot control or produce at will. It is so that they may come to know God, the One who is supremely *Other*, but to whom, nevertheless, all people are profoundly related and bound in love. For the Lord too, in an unfathomable and supernatural manner revealed in the Incarnation, is bone of our bone, flesh of our flesh, even to the point of going down with us into the grave.

LIVING WITH GLORY

Marriage is, before it is anything else, an act of contemplation. It is a divine pondering, an exercise in amazement. This is evident from the very start, from the moment a man and a woman first lay eyes on one another and realize they are in love. The whole thing begins with a wondrous *looking*, a helpless staring, an irresistible compulsion simply to behold. For suddenly there is so much to see! So much is revealed when two people dare to stand in the radiance of one another's love. And so there is a divine paralysis of adoration: Everything else stops, or at least fades into the background, and love itself takes center stage. Suddenly, for what seems the first time in life, one is presented physically and three-dimensionally with an object that is entirely worthy of one's wholehearted love and devotion. That is what "falling in love" means. Naturally one cannot believe one's eyes. That love should come embodied, encased in flesh, walking and talking and loving in return—for that we are never quite prepared. Of course we are programmed for it, to anticipate and to long for love to enter our lives in this dramatic and personal fashion, but that is not to say we are not bowled over when it actually happens. For we are skeptics by nature, and as much as we may want and even expect miracles to occur, we do not really believe in them. When the miracle of love erupts before our eyes, we cannot help being swept off our feet, dumbfounded, incapacitated for any other action or response except that of love itself: gazing, marveling, contemplating, loving.

When this event takes place between a man and a woman, it means that forever afterward these two will be doomed in the situation in which they shall have no business whatsoever in being together at all unless it is first and foremost the business of continuing this same wondrous gazing into one another's eyes, this helpless contemplation of the mystery of their love. For marriage, as simply as it can be defined, is the contemplation of the love of God in and through the form of another human being. It is spellbound fascination with the sheer incarnation of something so purely spiritual. Without this activity (which is no activity at all, really, but a heavenly stasis, a simple gazing into the depths of love), all the other motions and duties and activities of marriage will be empty. When a marriage loses this, when it loses the power to stop a couple in their tracks and arrest them into the rest of loving contemplation, when simple love for its own sake no longer holds center stage, then a marriage has lost its heart. To lose this simplest and most obvious thing of all is to lose everything.

Marriage is living with glory. It is living with an embodied revelation, with a daily unveiling and unraveling of the mystery of love in such a way that our intense yet shy curiosity about such things is in a constant state of being satisfied, being fed, yet without ever becoming sated. It is living with a mystery that is fully visible, with a flesh-and-blood person who can be touched and held, questioned and probed and examined and even made love to, to our heart's content, but who nevertheless proves to be utterly and impenetrably mysterious, infinitely contemplable.

BEING THERE

A marriage, or a marriage partner, may be compared to a great tree growing right up through the center of one's living room. It is something that is just there, and it is huge, and everything has been built around it, and wherever one happens to be going—to the fridge, to bed, to the bathroom, or out the front door—the tree has to be taken into account. It cannot be gone through; it must respectfully be gone around. It is somehow bigger and stronger than oneself. True, it could be chopped down, but not without tearing the house apart. And certainly it is beautiful, unique, exotic: but also, let's face it, it is at times an enormous inconvenience.

So there are many things that can be said about one's life's mate, but finally, irrevocably, the one definite thing that needs to be said is that he or she is always there. And that, while it may be common enough in the world of trees, is among us human beings a rather remarkable state of affairs.

Marriage is the most persistent and ineluctable reminder of the presence of other people in the world: that they are there, that they are real, and that they are wildly different from the imaginary beings who normally people our thoughts and fantasies. To be married is to be confronted intimately day after day with the mystery of life, of other life, of life outside of oneself. This is not the life of existentialism or of metaphysics or of Zen. It is more intrusively personal than Zen. It is life, human life as one has never seen it before, at closer range than one ever thought to get. The loved one simply is there, in a way that no other living thing in the world except oneself has ever really been there before. Even parents do not intrude and impinge upon one's adult life the way a spouse does, and it can be rather a surprise to discover that one is, after all, not alone. At night, in the morning, naked, over meals, in bath, and in bed, the partner is always there, there in body or there in spirit, there at the back of the mind and there in the pit of the heart. Although day-to-day married life may seem as natural and almost as automatic as breathing, yet there is a way in which the two partners never really do get used to one another, not in the way they are used to breathing. As autonomic, as tedious, as dreary as a marriage can become, there is nevertheless something in it that defies being taken for granted. The whole course of a couple's life together is fated to share that same odd quality of perfect naturalness united with perfect awkwardness—second nature combined with utter novelty—that characterized their first lovemaking.

In the long run what is most uncanny about marriage is not any sense of growing familiarity and comfortableness with the enormous reality of this other presence in one's life, but rather just the opposite: the growing strangeness. As the years roll by, all that happens is that the puzzle of time is added to the original enigma of love. Ten years, thirty years, fifty—it becomes more and more imponderable. There is just something so purely and untouchably mysterious in the fact of living out one's days cheek by jowl under the same roof with another being who always remains, no matter how close you manage to get, essentially a stranger. You know this person better than you have ever known anyone, yet often you wonder whether you know them at all. The sense of strangeness increases, almost, with the depth and security of the loved one's embrace.

What is this alien, unknowable place at the very heart of the one we love? Probably it is the place of our own familiarity with God. For one of the most profound ways in which the Lord touches us, and teaches us about Himself and His own essential *otherness,* is through the very limits He has placed upon our relationships with one another. It is an enormous source of human frustration that our need for intimacy far outstrips its capacity to be met in other people. Primarily what keeps us separate is our sin, but there is also another factor, which is that in each one of us the holiest and neediest and most sensitive place of all has been made and is reserved for God alone, so that only He can enter there. No one else can love us as He does, and no one can be the sort of Friend to us that He is.

Forming a relationship with us that is far deeper than anything we can possibly know among people is the way God has of challenging and inspiring us to yearn for this same divine depth in all of our human friendships. Were it not for the profound and intuitive knowledge of the Lord in our hearts, we could not know what depth of relationship is and would never miss or long for it on the human level. And so the very distance we feel from the person we love most dearly may be, paradoxically, a measure of the overwhelming closeness of God.

Out of Our Depth

Such closeness is not something we have chosen for ourselves, nor ever could have chosen, any more than we could have chosen to be alive in the first place. Such choices are, however, ones that we can grow into, and there is a sense in which they become more and more our own choices the older we get.

Marriage is one of the great steps we can take in the direction of choosing for ourselves what has really already been given to us: It is a choosing of the closeness of God, in the form of a close relationship with another person. It is a deliberate choosing of closeness over distance, of companionship over detachment, of relationship over isolation, of love over apathy, of life over death. It is not a choice that comes to us at all naturally. It can come only supernaturally, by the divine agency of love. For love is what makes choice possible. But more than that, it is what makes it possible for people to choose what is good for them, even though that is not their natural inclination.

That the natural human inclination is not toward good or toward love or toward depth of relationship is a fact that is absolutely fundamental to a proper appreciation of marriage. For if marriage is to be seen for the great miracle of grace that it is, what must first be seen is how much it goes against the grain of fallen human nature. Are there problems in marriage? Every one of them results from the partners trying desperately to renege, however subconsciously or surreptitiously, on a choice they have already made, a choice to which they have been led by love, and by love alone, as a man is blindfolded and led to the edge of a cliff, informed that he is standing beside his comfortable bed, and encouraged to lie down in it and relax. Love coaxes and even hoodwinks us into the making of a decision so radical that if left to our own devices we would never have entertained it for a moment. For it is a far stranger thing for two people to live together in love all their lives than not to. Like life itself, it involves a decision so staggering that it cannot really be made at all: It can only be grown into, at best consented to with ever-decreasing reluctance.

To put it simply, marriage is a relationship far more engrossing than we want it to be. It always turns out to be more than we bargained for. It is disturbingly intense, disruptively involving, and that is exactly the way it was designed to be. It is supposed to be more, almost, than we can handle. It was meant to be a lifelong encounter that would be much more rigorous and demanding than anything human beings ever could have chosen, dreamed of, desired, or invented on their own. After all, we do not even choose to undergo such far-reaching encounters with our closest and dearest friends. Only marriage urges us into these deep and unknown waters. For that is its very purpose: to get us out beyond our depth, out of the shallows of our own secure egocentricity and into the dangerous and unpredictable depths of a real interpersonal encounter.

And that, incidentally, is also what true religion is supposed to do. It is supposed to remind us that God is not an idol of our own making, not a human invention, not a concept or a theory or a projection or extension of ourselves, not a tool (any more than a marriage partner is a tool). No, the bizarre fact of the matter is that God, while invisible, really is *there—out* there, beyond our wildest dreams. He is a living Being with *personhood*, a true *Other* whom we can know with all the full-color intimacy and immediacy (and even more!) with which we know ourselves and the person we love, and with which we sense that we are known in return. To know the Lord is to be brought into a personal relationship so dramatic and overwhelming that marriage is only a pale image of it. Still, marriage is the closest analogy in earthly experience, and that is why the Bible so often uses the picture of a wedding, and of the bride and groom, to convey something of what it means for human beings to be united to God in love. The Christian faith, like marriage, aims at teaching us that the time when we are most ourselves is, paradoxically, when we are busy losing ourselves in another, when we are before the altar making vows of love and self-sacrifice, when we are out of our own depth and drowning in the deep waters of otherness. That is when we can begin to discover, experimentally, that others are as real as we are, and therefore begin to love them as we love ourselves and even as God so incredibly loves His people.

The very fact that creation has an objective reality and that other people have objective reality is meant to point us to the even more overwhelming reality of God. If the things He made are real and distinguishable in their separateness, then how much more Real and Other must be their Source? At the same time, one way we know of God's deep love for us is through the entirely undeserved compliment He has paid in regarding us as being every bit as real as He Himself is, even to the point of making it possible for us to share in His eternal life. In the Bible, indeed, our Lord has made it abundantly clear that He loves mankind so much that He Himself wants to marry them. He wants us to be His bride.

Body-Guarded Reality

First, however, He wants us to learn to pay this same undeserved and unqualified compliment to others, the high and magnanimous compliment of regarding others as being every bit as real and important as we are, which is to say, loving them as we love ourselves. This is the path of perfection the Lord has set in our hearts, and of all the experiments people have made in following it, none is more radical than that of marriage.

For it is no small thing, this experiencing of the fullest reality, at closest range, of another human being, this exercise of *living together.* It is no small thing to open our hearts and our arms and allow another to enter there, to grant to another person the same worth, the same consequence, the same existential gravity that we take for granted in ourselves. The fact is that our natural tendency is to treat people as if they were not "others" at all, but merely aspects of ourselves. We do not experience them as the overwhelming, comprehensive realities that we feel ourselves to be. Compared with us, they are not quite real. We see them as if through a haze, the haze of our own all-engulfing selfhood. We are constantly filtering others through the fine electronic mesh of our own private system of perception, so that what finally reaches our awareness and registers there is not usually a real person at all, but a sort of computer image, a reconstruction based on our personal programming and biases. We live in a heavily screened, body-guarded reality. Not much gets through the barbed wire, not much gets by the great bulldog of the ego. For truly to open our hearts to other people is to invite them into our own throne room and to sit them down on our very own throne, on the seat normally warmed by no one but ourselves. And to do that is to have the throne, the seat of the ego, rocked right off its foundations. Love is an earthquake that relocates the center of the universe.

It is true that we have never actually experienced, as Adam did, what it is like to be the only person on earth. And yet many of us live most of our lives as if this were indeed our situation, and that is why there is a kind of suffering known as "loneliness," a kind of suffering known as "alienation." People can be surrounded by other people and still be lonely and alienated, because they do not care, or do not know how, to get in touch anymore with the reality of others. After all, how tiring and intrusive other people can be! They heap us with expectations, demands, responsibilities, and any sense of significance in our own lives runs the risk of being swallowed up among the sheer numbers, the impossible teeming billions, of others in the world. We are expendable, it seems, so quickly replaced. Once we are gone, the rest of humanity will close over us the way water closes over a sinking stone. Is it any wonder if we seek some refuge from this terror of insignificance, from the crushing pressure of relationships, from the armies of other beings who would trek like locusts through the verdant pastures of our innermost souls? The need for such a refuge is met by the deliberate yet subliminal fantasy that we are all alone in the universe. And so we walk around with our heads in the clouds, pass people on the street as if they were telephone poles, look them straight in the eyes and hardly see them, and engage in conversations that are really only conversations with ourselves. Too often others are but the punctuation marks in the dry and windy monologues of our own self-centered existence.

This willful but unconscious dilution of the full reality of other people is at heart a dilution of the reality of God—a watering-down, that is, of reality Himself. For people are the consciousness of God in the world, the closest thing to Him in the physical realm, and a more vivid reminder than anything else in creation of His existence, His mystery, and His creative power. If man really is fashioned, more than anything else, in the image of God, then clearly it follows that there is nothing on earth so near to God as a human being. The conclusion is inescapable, that to be in the presence of even the meanest, lowest, most repulsive specimen of humanity in the world is still to be closer to God than when looking up into a starry sky or at a beautiful sunset.

Certainly that is why there is nothing in the New Testament about beautiful sunsets. The heart of biblical theology is a man hanging on a cross, not a breathtaking scene from nature. For the Bible is centrally concerned with love, and the wonders of nature (by comparison with the wonders of human relationships, healed and restored in Christ) touch only remotely on love. We cannot really love a sunset; we can love only a person. If we can be said to love things in nature at all, it is only by a sort of analogy with the love we bear for one another, and supremely for God Himself. Similarly with hate: We cannot really despise anything in nature with anywhere near the vehemence with which we can despise and reject one another and the Lord our God.

Other people, let's face it, confront us directly with the reality of love or hate that is in our hearts, in a way that all the beautiful sunsets in the world cannot do. It is as if every person we meet wears a strip of special litmus paper on his forehead, designed to reveal the presence of love or hate in us, and all the gradations in between. How shameful and embarrassing that would be! And yet it is precisely the situation we are in, and that is why everyone on earth bears a secret resentment toward everyone else, simply for being alive. We resent one another for revealing so accurately and so openly and so painfully the depth of our own lovelessness. It is a lovelessness that is not revealed in a starry sky, but only in the eyes of a fellow human being.

Admittedly, in people who have found in Christ the true power to love, this resentment of others may be residual, but it is present nonetheless, and those who do love are actually the very ones to whom this terrible truth is most obvious, and most obvious of all in themselves. And it is obvious too that this hidden antagonism toward others is fundamentally an antagonism toward God, an anger against Him for all the pain and the maddening obscurity of life. For how can we express anger toward an invisible Lord, how register a complaint against eternity? Since other people are as close as we can get to God in the physical world, since we cannot contact or get at Him any more directly, we settle for getting at Him through one another. And it works—it really does! How exciting to discover that the all-powerful God has a place of vulnerability, and that place is man! We cannot punch God in the nose, but we can punch another person. We cannot crucify God (at least, who could believe it if we did?), but we can crucify a man.

RIVALRY WITH GOD

Behind our fear and rejection of other people, then, it is vitally important to acknowledge our even deeper fear and rejection of God Himself. And just as we reduce the threat of others by slighting them and excluding them from our hearts, so also we slight and exclude the even greater threat of our God. If we have a tendency to behave as if we were the only, or the most important, person in the world, then how much more easily we can slip into the pattern of living that declares (whatever we may claim to believe) that our own existence is a more certain and significant fact than that of God's! Even religion itself may be manipulated into becoming an elaborate and systematic evasion of the living God, and ultimately a system of self-deification. What may have begun, like falling in love, as a deeply sincere and thrilling personal encounter can quickly degenerate into sterile self-centeredness. And so the worship of God may be changed into a quest for human fulfillment; obedience to God becomes enslavement to one's own dreams and passions; the kingdom of God is translated to mean a utopian society; and so on. In one way or another, religion may be used not to glorify God at all, but actually to shift the emphasis from God to man, and to do so in a way that drips with piety.

True religion can begin only with a profound acquiescence to one basic truth: that there is a God, and I myself am not He. But even when a man wakes up to this fact, it may not be the beginning of true faith in his life. It may, on the contrary, be the very point at which he launches a desperate and treacherous campaign to correct this infuriating imbalance between himself and his Lord, craving godhead for himself and calling this outrageous ambition by the name of "religion" or "faith" when actually it is just the opposite. The difference between religion and antireligion falls along the line between admiration (or worship) of the Deity and jealousy of Him, between the hunger to be *like* God and the hunger to *be* God. Religion seeks in holiness an antidote to sin and evil; irreligion seeks in superhumanness an antidote to God. In the pit of the human heart lies a seed of rivalry with God, a rivalry that in essence is a desire to usurp His position (so participating in the rebellion of Satan) but that in its most insidious form may take the shape of a religious belief subtly enshrining and justifying this very rebellion. Perfection is a haunting urge in us, yet not the perfection that grows from love, but a perfectionism motivated by pride and self-sufficiency. We would each like to be so perfect that it would not have been necessary for God to have created anyone else, nor ultimately for there to have been a God at all. In the frustration of our human impotence, we dream of being omnipotent—if not by right, then at least by default! Not that we ever articulate the wish quite this blatantly: But it is there nonetheless, a smoldering fantasy deep in our psyches, coloring our whole lives, the root of sin.

What is strangest of all about this secret ambition of ours to be God and to have the whole creation all to ourselves is that if it were true—that is, if you or I really were God, and had been from the beginning—it is highly unlikely that there would be any creation at all, and even less likely that we would ever have gone to the trouble of making a creature as miserable as ourselves. If we reject the true Lord, the holy and all-powerful Creator, how much more deeply and subliminally must we reject our own pitiable selves? The most glaring difference between me and the one Lord of the universe is probably this: that if I had been He, I would never have made anything. I would have washed my hands of the whole sticky business of otherness, and I wouldn't have lifted a finger to create one other blessed thing. Why bother, after all? Why burden myself with a creation, and especially with the creation of a troublesome brood of tiny impudent beings who would only turn around and spit in the face of their maker? No, I could have spared myself that little pleasure. I would have saved my breath. I would have been quite happy just to be all-in-all myself, to be the whole of humanity and divinity wrapped up in one sparkling, dynamic package, and to enjoy eternally my own self-existent infinitude.

WE ARE NOT ALONE

It ought to come as no surprise that marriage and religion have much in common. For both deal in the most direct way imaginable with the phenomenon of *otherness* in our lives, which is the core experience of what we call *relationship*. Both feed upon our peculiar sense of encounter with someone who is like us, resembling us in image, but who is not us. Both are committed to exploring, at enormous cost and risk, the farthest extremes and ramifications of this mystery of relationship, and the miracle called love that may only be found and generated at its heart. For given this natural bent of ours toward isolationism, how vital it is for us to know, to come to terms with, and to discover again and again the shattering truth that we indeed are not alone in the world! This is precisely the work of marriage, as it is of true religion: to remind us, daily, that we are not alone. We are not alone when it comes to other people, and neither are we alone when it comes to God.

However much we may wish at times to be left alone, it is not an option. It is the one thing that God and marriage refuse to allow us. They will not simply let us be. In one way or another, they are always on our backs, forever admonishing us that there is no such thing as life apart from relationship, which is to say, no life apart from the sharing of ourselves with another.

This is what is difficult about being a human being, about being alive: not life itself, but the sharing of it; not mere existence, but relationship. As persons, we have been called by God out of chaos and nothingness not simply to exist as the animals do, but to love. Man has been designed specifically for the forming of relationships based on love, and it is at this point that the success or failure of all the rest of creation hangs in the balance. The whole creation fell because of the failure, the sin, of one man. In the account of this event in Genesis, it is important to note that this sin of Adam was not so much an act of direct disobedience against God as it was an act of obedience to, or compliance with, another person. First Eve was seduced by the serpent into eating fruit from the forbidden tree, and then she "gave some to her husband…and he ate it" (Genesis 3:6). So the woman listened to the serpent, and the man listened to the woman, but no one listened to God; and afterwards the man blamed the woman, and the woman blamed the serpent, and all of them secretly blamed God.

In other words, original sin did not enter into the comparative simplicity of Adam's solitary life in Paradise, but rather into the complex world of relationships, of conflicting loyalties. The setting for this first sin was not so much the Garden of Eden, but the relationship among the man and the woman and the serpent. The essential task at which man failed was not that of living in peace with God, but of living in peace with another person before God, in the presence of temptation. That was, and remains to this day, the crux of religion, the place where all other spiritual work must begin. It is through one another that we sin, taking advantage of our neighbor as an occasion for falling, as an instrument for ignoring God, as a convenient excuse for our own weakness.

When Eve came into the world, she was not simply Eve: She was all human relationship. She was formed out of the very body of Adam, born out of him in order that she might enjoy an especially close bond with him, a bond that was to be not only the cornerstone of all future relations between people on earth, but *the* definition of humanity: "Male and female He created them" (Genesis 1:27). So special a thing was this in God's eyes that He saved it until last, until all the rest of His creative work was in place. The making of Eve was a sort of "up-level," a second stage added on to creation with a view to reproducing in the human race a reflection of God's own multipersonhood. Man was not to be an isolated creature, nor a whole horde of isolated creatures, but rather "one flesh," an entity somehow composite yet with no loss of individuality, united but without forfeiting the stupendous beauty and mystery of otherness: not man alone, but mankind.

Adam was a man alone, a singleton. But in the company of Eve he became a race, a corporate body, and only then did he become capable of mirroring the true and full life of God, which is the life of loving relationship. The message held in the mystery of the Trinity is that God is not a monistic singleton God, but rather a Three-in-One of whom loving relationship is the very essence, for He shares Himself even in the depths of His own being. Although He is the one and only Lord, He could not possibly exist alone, even prior to the creation, because God is love and love presupposes a relationship, a plurality (at least two) of persons. Without this plurality there could be no love. The very idea of sharing could never have existed, and therefore the Creation itself, that monumental act in which the Creator undertook to share Himself with creatures, could never have taken place. There are other religions that claim belief in one God, and still others that worship many gods. But only Christianity embraces the magnificent reality of the Trinity, of three divine persons subsisting in perfect unity in one Godhead. Only a God who lives with Himself in love can call upon a man and a woman to love one another, let alone command all people to love their enemies. This God alone embodies the power for gathering into the unity of love the vast multiplicity of mankind. He alone is at the same time the Creator, the Perfect Example, and the Transcender of personhood: Father, Son, and Holy Spirit.

Where We Hurt Most

Like God Himself, then, marriage comes with a built-in abhorrence of self-centeredness. In the dream world of mankind's complacent separateness, amidst all our pleasant little fantasies of omnipotence and blamelessness and self-sufficiency, marriage explodes like a bomb. It runs an aggravating interference pattern, an unrelenting guerrilla war against selfishness. It attacks people's vanity and lonely pride in a way that few other things can, tirelessly exposing the necessity of giving and sharing, the absurdity of blame. Angering, humiliating, melting, chastening, purifying, it touches us where we hurt most, in the place of our lovelessness. Dragging us into lifelong encounters that at times may be full of boredom, tension, unpleasantness, or grief, marriage challenges us to abandon everything for the sake of love.

For in the first place, love convinces a couple that they are the greatest romance that has ever been, that no two people have ever loved as they do, and that they will sacrifice absolutely anything in order to be together. And then marriage asks them to prove it. Marriage is the down-to-earth dimension of romance, the translation of a romantic blueprint into costly reality. It is the practical working out of people's grandest dreams and ideals and promises in the realm of love. It is one of God's most powerful secret weapons for the revolutionizing of the human heart. It is a heavy, concentrated barrage upon the place of our greatest weakness, which is our relationship with others. We cannot possibly, it is true, in any practical way maintain a commitment to every other person in the world: That is God's business, not ours. But marriage involves us synecdochically in this mystical activity of God's by choosing for us just one person, one total stranger out of all the world's billions, with whom to enter into the highest and deepest and farthest reaches of sacrificial, loving relationship.

It has been said that the secret to building a good fire is simply to rest one log against another. Marriage builds a good hot fire on the simple principle of resting one man and one woman up against each other in a hypostatic union of persons. "As iron sharpens iron," says the proverb, "so one person sharpens another," and the saying is nowhere more apt than in marriage. The key to it is what we have been referring to as "otherness": that strange encounter of separate identities as one person rubs up against another to produce an edge, to produce the flashing keenness of love. For even God is not a bachelor.

Naturally it is painful to be sharpened, painful to have one's dullness filed to a point. Yet at the same time it is a rich and warm and spellbinding adventure to live side by side with something that is that tough—harder than iron, hotter than fire, tougher even than hate—and to know that there is this one thing in life that one cannot get around, cannot fool, cannot escape being sharpened by. The whole world is being sharpened by love, but it is in the special fire of covenant relationships that the keenest and brightest edges are being honed. For we stand in the light of others, and that light reveals to us who we ourselves are. The light is brightest where the love is most intense, and the love is most intense where it is most practical, where the experiment in closeness is most intimate and daring.

What is most unique about the tenacious fidelity of marriage is that it allows for such a really brutal amount of sharpening to take place, yet in the gentlest way imaginable. Who ever heard of being sharpened against a warm, familiar body of loved flesh? Only the Lord could have devised such an awesomely tender and heartwarming means for men and women to be made into swords. Yet for all its gentleness, marriage is still a fire and a sword itself, a fire that brands and a sword that inflicts a wound far deeper than any arrow of Cupid. For it is a wound in a person's pride, in a place that cannot be healed, and from the moment a man and a woman first stand transfixed in one another's light they will begin to feel this wound of marriage opening up in them. The Lord God made woman out of part of man's side and closed up the place with flesh, but in marriage He reopens this empty, aching place in man and begins the process of putting the woman back again, if not literally in the side, then certainly at it: permanently there, intrusively there, a sudden lifelong resident of a space that until that point the man will have considered to be his own private territory, even his own body. But in marriage he will cleave to the woman, and the woman to him, the way his own flesh cleaves to his bones.

Just so, says the Lord, do I Myself desire to invade your deepest privacy, binding you to Me all your life long and even into eternity with cords of blood.

a winged locomotive

Love

How beautiful you are, my darling!
Oh, how beautiful! ...
You have stolen my heart
with one glance of your eyes.

SONG OF SONGS 4.1, 9

Love

IN THE DUNGEON

In marriage, one of the deepest and most ethereal mysteries in all of life is demystified before our very eyes. For when we get married, love itself comes to live with us. That thing we have been chasing ever since we were old enough to believe (however naively) that it must or could be sought, has taken off all its clothes and stretched itself out on our very own bed and announced that it is here to stay. Suddenly the thing we believed to be characterized above all else by its elusiveness turns out to be not elusive at all, but just the opposite. That which was unapproachable becomes that which cannot be gotten rid of. What was most glamorous and exciting seems to insist, now, on being the most ordinary thing in the world. It is like the philosophical question about the dog chasing the car: What happens if he catches it? Marriage faces us squarely with the problem of what to do with love once we have finally caught it.

Or rather, once it has caught us. For marriage is a trap. It is a trap of pure love. The love is so pure, so intense, that it can be like a big iron gate that clangs shut behind us. And there we are.

Imprisoned, of our own free will, in the dungeon of marriage. And the one and only key has been handed over to our partner, a total stranger, to swallow.

No prison is darker than that of an imprisoning human relationship, and no marriage can escape without tasting to some extent of this sense of imprisonment. For this is just the sort of thing love loves to do. It loves to back us into a corner. It loves to rip out our independence like a rug from under our feet, and then stand back and watch what we will do. It loves to see us take enormous risks for its own sake, only to turn around and leave us in the lurch. There is perhaps nothing in the world so treacherous, nor ultimately so cool and calculating and intractable, as love. How infuriatingly irresponsible it can be, sweeping people off their feet and turning around their whole lives as casually as if they were leaves in an autumn breeze! Many people are very surprised to find out what love can be like underneath its charming exterior.

Of course, love has its own purposes. And those purposes involve nothing short of a worldwide revolution: a revolution in which everything in sight will be turned into pure love. That is what it has in mind. And that is why it employs this cruel and drastic strategy of backing people into corners, squeezing them into impossible situations in which the only way they can ever hope to pry themselves free is by responding in kind with love, allowing themselves to be made more and more loving, to be made the tools and pawns of love, and learning to love what love has done to them. When the prison door of love clangs shut, the only thing to do is to become more in love than ever. There is just no other way to get out of it.

So, we are caught in the steel trap of marriage, and we do a lot of squirming and struggling, but over and over we must wake up to the fact that there is only one way to get untrapped, and that is to relax and start learning more about love than we ever wanted to know. Time and again love throws its pail of cold water in our faces, patiently explaining once more that it is not at all what we thought it was. But again and again we fail to get the hang of it, or else fail to take it at its word.

Is there anything that irks us more than this whimsical little dictator called love? Is even hate more irritating, more intrusive and unsettling? At least hate has a quality of predictability to it, a dependable sameness. But love is a chameleon, forever changing colors, scurrying away under rocks. It seems to enjoy wriggling out of one's grasp. It puffs itself up until it is the most real and dazzling and important thing in the world and then suddenly fizzles and deflates, blending back into the pale desert landscape of ordinary humdrum life. That, at least, is how the great majority of lovers seem to experience it.

Probably the most frequent comment couples may be heard to make about marriage is that "it has its ups and downs." The ups are the times when love is plain as day, big as life, and fully visible (visible, that is, to the conscious mind and the feelings). But the downs are the times when love goes undercover, incommunicado, so that there may appear to be nothing left of it at all. So commonplace is this observation about the ups and downs of marriage that one wonders whether it shouldn't be written right into the vows. But of course, it is: "for better, for worse…"

If life itself is full of vicissitudes, then the same is even more true of marriage, for marriage embraces two lives at once, two lives so extraordinarily interconnected that only God, as Jesus tells us in Mark 10:9, could ever untangle or sunder them. So delicate and complex is this balance of lives and wills that it can be accomplished only by sleight of hand, by the prestidigitation of love. People have to be taught love in spite of themselves. It has to be smuggled into their lives when they are not looking. Love has a way of coming to people behind their backs, of sneaking up, for instance, at a time in their lives when they may be particularly incomprehensible to themselves.

There is always this now-you-see-it-now-you-don't quality to love, as there is to any spiritual reality, to anything so vast and profound that it can never quite be taken in by the human mind and senses. Love does its greatest work at night, underground, often in disguise, and at lightning speed—so fast that no one can possibly keep up with it. Even when we do catch a glimpse of love, it is still miles ahead of us. It leaves us spinning as it hurtles by, leaves us in a cloud of dust. We cannot catch hold of it; rather, it catches hold of us. It is unpredictable, nonrational, supernatural. It is not accounted for in the theory of evolution. We can see some of the effects of love in our lives, but we can never see them all, and we cannot see love itself. It is of the very essence of love that it be invisible and incomprehensible and a million light-years beyond us, and so much greater than we are that we swoon at its touch.

Who therefore does not resent the vast, total claim that alien love lays over our hearts? For love is like death: What it wants is all of us. And who has not been frightened almost to death by love's dark shadow gliding swift and huge as an interstellar shark, like a swimming mountain, through all the deepest waters of our being, through depths we never knew we had? It is not love unless it overwhelms and at some point petrifies us. For there is a sting of love, a bite, and it is fatal. A man who has been bitten by love will die for what he loves, and he may die utterly against his will. For his will (if all has gone well) will have been trapped, held as in an iron vise, totally possessed by love.

A New Stage of Childhood

This is not to say that love is actually without freedom. Indeed, in the initial experience of falling in love it is the freedom itself that can be so positively terrifying, the sense of being faced as never before with the sheer magnitude of the repercussions inherent in one's own free decisions. For the choice of a marriage partner (combined, of course, with the choice to get married in the first place; the two cannot really be separated) is one of the very freest choices we make as human beings. We may not perceive the true extent of our freedom when we are right in the midst of the process. There are even people who prefer to think, after the fact, that they were actually *pressured* into their marriage vows, or that circumstances simply overwhelmed them, or that they lost their heads and became incapable of rational thought! Nevertheless, considering the clear-eyed, swaggering panache of lovers, and the radical whoosh and daring with which they set about completely reorganizing their lives around the loved one and the impending wedding, surely most other times in life appear by comparison the very opposite of liberty. Love pumps around spontaneity like adrenaline and spends freedom like a fat bankroll. You can practically live on love.

It is no secret that there is this heady, breathtaking freedom in love, but how many realize that the marrying kind is the headiest of all? In a person about to be married there is a quality of foot-loose derailment, as if an old rusty locomotive had suddenly sprouted wings and soared away from its tracks. Being engaged is like entering a new stage of childhood, right down to the feeling of strange new chemicals being released into the body. It is, in fact, like having a *new body*, like being a brand-new creature just emerged from a cocoon, with shining skin not quite dry. It is like a baptism. The world is so *bright*, and this crazy new body is so incredibly *sensitive* to everything. It is one thing to be a new creature as a baby, without any sense of self-consciousness. But it is something else when this happens to an adult. One stumbles around, lumbers, cranes, reels. And what are those ponderous appendages on one's back, those preposterous, unwieldy contraptions that keep lifting one up into the air?

It's wonderful, sure, but also fearsome and unnerving, and so awesomely freeing that most people go through a desperate struggle to try to locate the switch that will somehow shift their minds and hearts onto automatic pilot, so that they might disclaim all future responsibility for their actions during this bizarre period. For always in love there is an immense and impossible decision to make, and there can be no real rest until it is made. It is like a pilot being faced with the decision to try to make a dead-stick landing of a jumbo jet in a cornfield. Love cannot circle around forever; it demands resoluteness, wholehearted commitment. Never satisfied with just a little bit of a person's heart, love wants the whole thing, and is forever pushing toward the brink.

So there is a sense of emergency, of impending cataclysm, of needing to bring all of the senses and every ounce of alertness to bear on a situation that could hardly be more volatile and that could actually make or break an entire life. For it is in the nature of love to be climactic. It is in the nature of love to bring the whole tangled plot of one's life to a single focus, to a single pointed question, a single decision, a single momentous coincidence of energies. There is nothing the least bit vague or abstract about it.

One does not love an abstraction; one loves the particular shape of a smile or the unique inflection of a voice, and no other voice and no other smile will do. Love is always precise, always so terrifyingly and exultantly explicit. The way to know it, in fact, is that it is the only thing that is that way. Everything else is blundering in the dark. But in love there is a law of gravity, an attraction to a single center. There is an obviousness about true love, an illuminatedness, a particularity and a certainty. To doubt it is to be plunged into darkness and confusion. But to believe in and accept it is to be filled with light. There is really nothing else like it. Few other decisions in life will be anywhere near as crucial as the decision to love or not to love. And once made, there can be no reneging.

But if getting married is a terrible decision to have to make in the first place, it can be an even more terrible one to live with. For the tremendous new freedom created by love does not grind to a halt (contrary to popular belief) on the wedding day. Instead, marriage turns out to be only the door into a whole can of worms of freedom, romantic love only a trap door that tumbles one willy-nilly into the desperately long free fall of true love, the footloose extravaganza of covenant. Being married is being on a hot tin roof of freedom, being in a place where love never sleeps. For love is restless by nature, continually searching, probing the depths, seeking tirelessly to enlarge the heart and to exploit to the fullest the endless possibilities of human liberty. To be married is not to be taken off the front lines of love but rather to be plunged into the thick of things. It is to be faced, day in and day out, with the necessity of making over and over again, and at deeper and deeper levels, that same terrifyingly momentous and impossible decision that one could never have made without being head over heels in love and out of one's mind with trust and faith. This is not resignation to a fate, but the free and spontaneous embracing of a gift, of a challenge, and a destiny.

Is it any wonder if people cannot take the pressure? It is a pressure that can be handled only by love, and in ever-increasing doses. Marriage involves a continuous daily renewal of a decision that, since it is of such a staggering order as to be humanly impossible to make, can be made only through the grace of God.

KISMET OR GRACE?

Often the question is raised as to whether falling in love is a matter of fate or coincidence. We wonder whether there is one special person for us, or whether given just the right circumstances we might equally well fall in love with any of a number of suitable candidates, or indeed with anyone at all.

A moment's reflection will suggest that, however titillating this question may be, it is really no question at all, for the appearance of two distinct alternatives is purely sophistical. Even if two people are destined from before their births to fall in love, surely some sort of coincidence is still necessary to bring them together. But on the other hand, if it is true that any two people may fall in love, given a suitable coincidence, then what is to say that this special set of circumstances known as coincidence has not been predetermined? After all, it is not as if circumstances can ever be considered as being external to the people concerned; on the contrary, the people, inseparable from all the baggage of their peculiar personalities and unique histories, are the circumstances. Fate and coincidence, it turns out, are names for the same thing. The door of coincidence turns upon the hinges of fate.

Either way, the great mystery is that one cannot fall in love at will. It is one of those things that just happens, and whether the mechanism that makes it happen be termed kismet or coincidence, accident or grace, we are nevertheless at its mercy. Even freedom, true freedom, cannot be manufactured in the depths of the human will but can be bestowed only as a gift. The train schedule of love runs on its own sweet time.

What is interesting, however, about this question of the fortuitousness of love, of whether it turns upon fate or coincidence, is that it is seriously asked only by those who are not yet in love, or not deeply in love, or who in fact have no idea what love is. These are the sort of people who like to ponder whether the lover they have found might be only one of any number of possibilities. But the person who is truly in love, by contrast, couldn't care less about other possibilities, just as one who has found the Truth takes no interest in "other truths." For the one who believes and for the one who loves, there is no other truth and there is no other love.

So real love is always fated. It has been arranged from before time. It is the most meticulously prepared of coincidences. And fate, of course, is simply the secular term for the will of God, and coincidence for His grace.

VISIONARY EXPERIENCE

Does not this fact—that love has been willed by God from eternity—take something away from its freshness and spontaneity? Certainly not! The essential characteristic of love, in fact, is what might be termed its "deus ex machina" aspect: the sense of something being there, quite suddenly and surprisingly, that was never there before. Something *created,* brand-new, so different and innovative that it succeeds in resetting the entire course of lives. One of the ways we know that love is from God, and that it is love, is that it always comes in a form and a manner we never could have anticipated. It comes out of the blue. For it is grace, pure and free, one of the most spectacular ways God has of pouring Himself out

upon people, exploding into their lives with breathtaking unexpect-
edness and bringing about sweeping renewal and transformation.

To fall in love actually means (whether or not a person cares to
admit this) to have a revelation from God. It is to receive from
Him a new vision as to the true nature of things and new insight
into the power and potential of life. But right away the lover has a
decision to make, a decision as to how much he is willing to let his
life be governed by a vision. To go forward from love into marriage
is to take a step of faith. It is to stake life upon a spiritual experience. There is no entering into the grace of marriage except
through the grasping of a whole new understanding of what love
itself means.

Obviously, this is not something we can do for ourselves. It is
a transcendent experience, a God-given vision that happens to
come to us through the medium of one particular special person.
And then we stand up with this one person and make a public declaration concerning the absolutely dramatic and convincing nature
of this vision we have had. So earth-shattering an experience has
this been that it seems entirely natural to give ourselves to it totally,
to vow right then and there to dedicate the rest of our lives to the
pursuit, exploration, testing, enjoying, and continual renewal of
this vision. It is an experiment, certainly—but an experiment that
will be totally invalid unless we stake our very lives upon the out-
come. We vow that we have had a visionary experience that will
enable us to love "until death do us part." We have stood on the
mountain, seen the new land, and become convinced that it is
worth setting out for. If we stop loving before death, if we abandon the pilgrimage at any point, then what we will have done is to
regress into a belief that there never was any mountain or vision of
a new land, and that love (at least that particular love) is no enduring reality but rather a passing fancy, an illusion or a mistake or a

matter of mere whim and emotion and circumstance. We will have shattered and rejected and invalidated one of the deepest spiritual experiences of our entire lives.

That is what is so distressing about divorce: It separates the divorcé not only from his mate but in many ways from his own religion. And this tends to be true, oddly enough, no matter what sort of religion a person happens to hold to. Even a religion of pure self-seeking and hedonism runs aground on the tragedy of divorce. The popular modern notion that partners can separate amicably, and even be better friends apart than when they were living together, is a preposterous myth. The very fact that separation takes place presupposes unpleasantness and hostility.

Having said this, it must also be recognized that separation may sometimes be a preferable hostility, and actually a more acceptable one to God, than the continuance of a marriage in the face of chronic and unresolved abuse. In those cases, divorce may be the lesser of two evils.

Whatever the particular circumstances, the fact remains that there can never be any retreat from marriage without the severest of consequences. For the vision that love opens up to us is so sweet and marvelous and transcendent that nothing else can begin to compare with it. Everything is dust and emptiness compared with one quick tip-of-the-tongue taste of love, let alone of the banquet of marriage. Is it any wonder that some people will do everything in their power to keep love away from them? For we all know instinctively that love is like some violent revolutionary, head stuffed with wild dreams instead of brains, a dangerous idealist who would like nothing better than to grab hold of us and shake us right down to our boots, overthrowing all our old ideas and ambitions, drastically renovating our hearts from the ground up, filling us with entirely new motives for living. To give in to such a force, for one moment, is to be quite, quite swept away. Give love an inch and it will take our whole lives, and it will all happen like lightning, in the twinkling of an eye.

Beating the Ego at Its Own Game

This is what makes marriage such a thrilling enterprise: that it has the power, much more than other more obviously disruptive forces, to change the entire course of a life. Some people go into marriage thinking that they will not have to change much, or perhaps only a little bit along lines that are perfectly foreseeable and within their control. Such people are in for a rough ride. When the terrifying and inexorable process of change sets in, they dig in their heels and refuse to budge, and the ensuing tug-of-war wreaks havoc in every department of their previously comfortable existence.

Marriage, even under the very best of circumstances, is a crisis—one of the major crises of life—and it is a dangerous thing not to be aware of this. Whether it turns out to be a healthy, challenging, and constructive crisis, or a disastrous nightmare, depends largely upon how willing the partners are to be changed, how malleable they are. Yet ironically, it is some of the most hardened and crusty and unlikely people in the world who plunge themselves into the arms of marriage and thereby submit in almost total naïveté to the two most transforming powers known to the human heart: the love of another person and the gracious love of God. So be prepared for change! Be prepared for the most sweeping and revolutionary reforms of a lifetime.

Generally speaking, there is really only one other event that normally involves a person in a more thoroughgoing, far-reaching program of personal reforms, and that is a religious conversion.

When speaking of love and marriage, then, we would do well to keep in mind that this is the order of events we have to deal with. We are not simply moving in with someone we think it might be fun to live with. Rather, we are giving our prior assent to a whole chain reaction of trials, decisions, transformations, and personal cataclysms that, once they are done with us, may leave us not only changed almost beyond recognition, but marked nearly as deeply as by a religious conversion. And this is just as it ought to be. Love being the most potent of forces, it is hardly surprising that the most overwhelming experiences of life should be those of being in love—first with God and then with another human being.

There is no trick of a magician or spell of a witch doctor, no drug or mesmerism or bribery or torture or coercion that can compare in power with the force for change unleashed in the human breast through the touch of love. Love is the greatest of teachers, for there is no authority more compelling, no power more hypnotically transfixing, no counsel more wise, no message we are more longing to hear, no other master for whom it is easier to give up absolutely everything in order to follow and obey. When love knocks at the door, what sort of man does not drop whatever he is doing at once and come running? Even if we are one of those who stubbornly refuse to open up to love, still we cannot help crouching there at the other side of the keyhole, obscurely begging him not to go away, not to leave us alone (however much we may appear on the surface to want just that) but rather imploring and daring him in desperate, pitiful incoherence to find some way, any way, of breaking down our defenses, of pouring into us his glorious light.

Little wonder that we are fascinated with stories of love affairs, of people falling in love and being lifted out of the rut of humdrum existence, just as we are fascinated with stories of enlightenment and religious conversion. Of course, war is also a fascinating subject—but even war has never been, and never will be, as popular a spectacle as love! For war specializes in the whole-sale destruction of human life, whereas love, building up and celebrating life, specializes in the destruction of something far more powerful and unyielding than life itself, and that is the human ego. Love is spiritual warfare. It is no great feat to crush physical bodies: The flesh is frail and vulnerable, and its lifeblood all too easily spills out. But to locate a chink in the ego or the innermost self, as true love does, and to give pride a run for its money—there is an awesome feat! There is power!

How does love do it? How does love succeed again and again against astounding odds in coaxing people out of the secure dark-ness of their selfishness and into the humility and exposure of its own searing light? One explanation that may be offered, at the risk of sounding facile, is that love beats the ego at its own game. As the only quality that exists for and of itself alone and not in reac-tion against anything else, love turns out to be the only legitimate egoism, the purest manifestation of selfhood. In fact, it is the only state in which self can really exist. When the illegitimate self, the one that is founded upon human pride and illusion, comes up against the real thing, it cannot stand. It has found what it has been struggling all along to be and so crumbles with shame, relief, joy, realization. No more is it afraid of losing itself, for it has been found. Love wins over selfishness by actually making the whole concept of self obsolete, or at least by redefining it out of all recog-nition. For it is the special magic of love to demonstrate convincingly that the real goal of self, which is total self-sufficiency, can be achieved only by way of total self-sacrifice. Only love is completely self-sufficient, for only love has nothing whatsoever to lose in spilling itself out, since that is its very nature. Only love is so inwardly strong and deeply confident of itself that it does not ever need to retaliate, even against its bitterest enemies. Love alone stands alone, through having already surrendered everything.

Love attacks and destroys pride, therefore, simply by eliminating the need for it. Love creates the only safe ground upon which all the bristling weaponry of self-assertion may begin to be surrendered. What use is there in asserting the self if the self is already loved, fully and unreservedly, and not because of but in spite of anything it might do? What is there left to assert? When the self knows that it is already accepted, unconditionally, there is no need anymore for it to preoccupy itself with advancing its own claims or with trying to create the conditions that might make it worthy of being loved. As long as the self is consumed in the struggle to make itself lovely, it cannot love. First it must come to the end of its own resources, for the power to love derives purely and solely from the knowledge that one is already loved in return. The energy for love flows not out of any effort but simply from being loved.

And so the best marriages and the deepest relationships with God grow out of the startling discovery that there is nothing one can do to earn love, and even more startling, that there is also nothing one can do to unearn it, or to keep oneself from being loved. This is a religious awakening that is utterly different from any other religious experience, no matter how profoundly spiritual it may seem. It is the recognition of the true self in the simple discovery that one is loved. "How beautiful you are, my darling! Oh, how beautiful!" say the words of the fourth chapter of the Song of Songs. "You have stolen my heart with one glance of your eyes." They are the words of God Himself speaking with outrageous intimacy to the human soul.

Does a man remember the first time he held in his arms the strange woman who was to be his wife, and heard her say that he was loved? Did he understand, or did he dare even to believe it? More astounding still, did he realize then that those words issued not only from the woman herself, but from the Lord? Did he sense that it was really God telling him that He loved him, reassuring the man that it was all right for him to exist and to be himself, because while he might not be perfect, God's love for him was, and that was all that mattered? Surely there must be some stirring of that realization, however submerged it may be, whenever a man and a woman fall in love. Surely the love of others is intended to be one of the clearest of all signs to us that we are indeed loved by God. For whoever truly loves, loves the Lord, and whoever is loved, is loved by the Lord.

In this way, the love between a husband and wife is a participation in the love of God for the whole human race. Anyone who has been initiated into this miracle of married love can walk down a crowded street and peer into the unfamiliar face of each stranger, whether man or woman, and participate in the secret thrilling knowledge that each one of them is capable of being loved rapturously by another human being even as oneself is loved by one's own mate. Each stranger may be seen from the dazzling perspective of holding an absolutely irreplaceable spot in another's heart, of being potentially just as special and unique a person to someone else as one's own wife or husband is to oneself. When a person has loved, but especially when he has been loved, everyone in the world becomes more lovable.

So liberating is this miracle of loving and being loved that it is something of which a husband and wife will take great joy in reminding one another. Indeed, one of the most important tasks for a couple to fulfill is this work of telling one another their love, which at heart is a wonderful reminder that they each are loved by God. This will not always be a pleasant or an easy task: Sometimes, to be sure, when a wife says, "I love you," it is something that a husband does not want to hear, at times something that he almost cannot bear to hear. He is tired of hearing it. He doesn't want to think about what it means. He doesn't want to let go of whatever prevents him from accepting it. He doesn't have the time or the energy to make a response. He doesn't want to be bothered with it. It is one more responsibility he can do without. He is not in the mood to be loved, let alone to love in return.

Still, in spite of all resistance, the words of love are important. It is important that they be heard, and it is important that they be spoken, out loud, no matter how painful this hearing and this speaking might be. It is a marvelous thing when love comes bubbling up like tears in the throat as one is gripped by a sudden stabbing realization of the other's beauty and goodness, of how incredibly precious this person is. But more imperative still than the speaking of love when it cannot be held in is the speaking of it when it can, even if the speaking seems almost impossible, even if the words must be choked out like some piece of foreign matter in the esophagus that has to be coughed up before one can breathe again freely. Perhaps the time to speak will be a time of strife and hurt, or perhaps a time when one or the other's deepest and most incorrigible human weakness shows painfully through, like a splintered bone protruding out of the skin. At such times, like an apology or a confession, an "I love you" can drop thunderous and unexpected and shockingly bright and innocent from the lips, coming as a profound surprise even to the one who speaks it. For it is sin, every bit as much as beauty or goodness, that occasions real love, and the thing that is most amazing about a word of love is how often, in spite of all circumstances, it does indeed spring from the place of genuine love, managing somehow to be always true, always new, always startling.

Granted, there are bound to be times when it rings hollow, when it seems to emerge from the mouth of an unrepentant swindler, a phony, a dead man. But by and large a word of love is a most remarkable little thing, a confession that perhaps more than any other sentence one can utter (including even "I believe") constrains the speaker to *mean* it. For it has the nature of a personal confession, and to say it without sincerity is a self-accusation, a heartrending conviction, every time. And yet not to say it at all is a worse conviction. Reflecting on this for a moment, it should be evident that the life of faith is full of such words, words that demand to be spoken and meant, words that on the outside may appear hollow, but the very speaking of which hallows them, fills them with life and depth. Is this not the case with all the hollow, meaningless language of prayer, the speaking of our love to God? Words are dead and empty things until they are filled, and the only way they can be filled is to say them and to mean them from the heart. And even then continual invoking may be required before their meaning begins to swell and to sink in like a long, long rain into parched roots. For the tongue is a pen, that pressing deeply enough (and whether for good or for evil), will write upon the heart.

FROM THE TIME OF MAN'S INNOCENCY

And so we must learn to love with our mouths and voices, as well as with our eyes, flesh, hearts, brains, and with everything we have, right down to our toenails. There is not anything about us that cannot love, and that is not called to love, and that is not destined to be turned, conformed, and reduced to pure love. It is the priceless deposit left by the burning away of selfishness.

Love is more than the way we practice for the world to come: It *is* the world to come. It is all that we shall be allowed to take into the kingdom of God. Even marriage itself, after all, is to be excluded: "When they rise from the dead, men and women do not marry," taught Jesus; "no, they are like the angels in Heaven" (Mark 12:25). Yet whatever may be the ultimate fate of marriage as an institution, we may be sure that the love that flowers within it will never be lost. Not the smallest amount of trust, patience, understanding, or self-giving that marriage teaches a couple to have and to practice on earth will go to waste in the kingdom. All of it will be necessary; every little gram of love will be important.

But how can the love of a marriage survive if marriage itself passes away? Will there be no reunion of husband and wife in eternity? It is difficult to imagine a Heaven in which lovers would be separated or would fail to recognize one another, or in which love would somehow be divorced from the reality of individual loved ones. On the contrary, we believe that Christian love depends implicitly upon the mystery of individual personhood, that the highest love can never find its focus in anything abstract, but only in the particularity of a person. What is it about marriage, then, that could possibly exclude it from Heaven?

Considering the rich imagery of weddings and marriage throughout the Bible, it seems more probable that far from there being *no* marriage in Heaven, what Jesus must really have been getting at is that Heaven will be *all* marriage. Indeed, in earthly marriage we may detect the sign and promise that in eternity everyone is to be married to everyone else in some transcendent and unimaginable union, and everyone will love everyone else with an intensity akin to that which now is called "being in love," and which impels individual couples to spend their whole lives together. In this way Christian marital love is (or should be) as close as we are likely to experience to being a piece of Heaven on earth, for it is a true leftover from Paradise. It is something that, in the beautiful words of the *Anglican Prayer Book,* has been "instituted from the time of man's innocency."

THREE

the wild frontier

Intimacy

Has not the Lord made them one?
In flesh and spirit they are his.

—Malachi 2:15

Intimacy

TWO INTO ONE

Marriage is the closest bond that is possible between two human beings. That, at least, was the original idea behind it. It was to be something unique, without parallel or precedent. In the sheer sweep and radical abandon of its commitment, it was to transcend every other form of human union on earth, every other covenant that could possibly be made between two people. Friendship, parent-child, master-pupil—marriage would surpass all these other bonds in a whole constellation of remarkable ways, including equality of the partners, permanent commitment, cohabitation, sexual relations, and the spontaneous creation of blood ties through simple spoken promises. As it was originally designed, marriage was a union to end all unions, the very last word (and the first) in human intimacy. Socially, legally, physically, emotionally, every which way, there is just no other means of getting closer to another human being, and never has been, than in marriage.

Such extraordinary closeness is bought at a cost, and the cost is nothing more nor less than one's own self. No one has ever been married without being shocked at the enormity of this price and at the monstrous inconvenience of this thing called intimacy that suddenly invades one's life. At the wedding a bride and groom may have gone through the motions of the candle-lighting ceremony, blowing out their own flames and lighting one central candle in place of the two. But the touching simplicity of this ritual has little in common with the actual day-to-day pressures of two persons being merged into one. It is a different matter when the flame that must be extinguished is no lambent flicker of a candle but the blistering inferno of self-will and independence. There is really nothing else like this lifelong cauterization of the ego that must take place in marriage. All of life is, in one way or another, humbling. But there is nothing like the experience of being humbled by another person and by the same person day in and day out. It can be exhausting, unnerving, infuriating, disintegrating. There is no suffering like the suffering involved in being close to another person. But neither is there any joy nor any real comfort at all outside of intimacy, outside the joy and the comfort that are wrung out like wine from the crush and ferment of two lives being pressed together.

What happens to a couple when they fall in love, when they pitch headlong into this winepress of intimacy, is not simply that they are swept off their feet; more than that, the very ground they are standing on, the whole world and ground of their own separate selves, is swept away. A person in love cannot help becoming, in some sense, a new person. After all, even to stand for five minutes beside a stranger in a supermarket lineup, without exchanging one word, is to be drawn irresistibly, uncomfortably, enigmatically into the dizzying vortex of another human life. It is to be subtly swayed, held, hypnotized, transfixed—moved and influenced in myriad ways, subliminal and seldom analyzed, but nonetheless potent. But marriage takes this same imponderable magnetism and raises it to an infinite power. The very next step in human closeness, beyond marriage, would be just to scrap the original man and woman and create one new human being out of the two.

But this is exactly what happens (both in symbol and in actuality) in the birth of a child! Eventually the parents die, leaving the child as a living sign of the unthinkable extremity of union that took place between two distinct lives. The two became one: "Has not the LORD made them one? In flesh and spirit they are His. And why one? Because He was seeking godly offspring" (Malachi 2:15).

THE WILD FRONTIER

Marriage partners may be thought of as the astronauts of society—the daring explorers who do all the test-flying in a sort of ongoing experiment in the most radical fringes of human relations. Naturally there are many crashes, many casualties in this stratosphere of intimacy. It is a most dangerous profession and one with a high rate of burnout. It is demanding, draining, and often dreary work, and unlike space exploration the rewards it offers do not seem very glamorous. There will be no ticker-tape parades for the good wife or husband, and most couples actually have a tendency to avoid the very aspects of their work that do offer the greatest rewards. Particularly are they prone to resent all the time they must "waste" with one another, and after the first year or so of marriage they begin to have great difficulty believing that the lavish interpersonal extravagance that characterized their courtship might actually still be allowed, let alone be a necessary or a glorious thing.

Accordingly, great amounts of energy are channeled into other concerns, into friendships and social life, into careers, into the raising of offspring (godly or otherwise), into every conceivable cause except the cause of marriage itself. For what possible practical use could there be in continuing that systematic and unrelenting invasion of privacy that is the heart and soul, the rocket fuel, of a loving relationship? Everywhere else, throughout society, there are fences, walls, burglar alarms, unlisted numbers, the most elaborate precautions for keeping people at a safe distance. But in marriage all of that is reversed. In marriage the walls are down, and not only do the man and woman live under the same roof, but they sleep under the same covers. Their lives are wide open, and as each studies the life of the other and attempts to make some response to it, there are no set procedures to follow, no formalities to stand on. A man and a woman face each other across the breakfast table, and somehow through a haze of crumbs and curlers and mortgage payments they must encounter one another. That is the whole purpose and mandate of marriage. All sorts of other purposes have been dreamed up and millions of excuses invented for avoiding this central and indispensable task. But the fact is that marriage is grounded in nothing else but the pure wild grappling of soul with soul, no holds barred. There is no rule book for this, no law to invoke except the law of love.

So while marriage may present the appearance of being a highly structured, formalized, and tradition-bound institution, in fact it is the most free and raw and unpredictable of all human associations. It is the outer space of society, the wild frontier. While it may seem to be just one more cog in the machinery of social order, in point of fact nothing else in secular society comes even close to the seriousness, the all-pervasiveness, the indissolubility and sheer daring of marriage. Indeed this little unit, bonded together by these preposterously simple and unique and revolutionary vows, is the beating heart of society itself. For there is no society without it. Without these odd male-female dyads, these unlikely little pairs of folk who (whether they like to admit it or not) have died to one another in love, everything else in society would fall apart.

It would be as if suddenly the laws of physics were such that two dissimilar atoms could no longer exist in conjunction with one another with any degree of permanence; that being the case, there could be no matter, no universe, no anything. Everything hinges upon conjugality, and marriage, as the most extreme case of human conjunction, represents par excellence that one mysterious binding force in human relationships upon which all others depend. It is the smallest of all organizations, with never more than two members, yet if there were only one such organization of two in the whole world, its significance would suddenly become radiantly apparent. Surely such a couple would be more famous than Shakespeare, the Beatles, the Pope, or a man with a brain transplant. As it is, the fact that marriages are more common and numerous than the stars takes nothing away from their importance. Clubs, fraternities, communes, communities, and nations—all take their basic cue and pattern from the model of marriage, and yet each draws on only a fraction of that transcendent force for human cohesion that is present in its totality (or most nearly so) only in the marriage unit.

It is no wonder that people love weddings. A wedding is one of the very few occasions when the formation of a true and lasting bond between two human beings may be witnessed. In no other sphere (be it business, politics, or even friendship) is the forming of a voluntary bond of partnership so real or decisive, so permanent, nor so clear and simple. Marriage is the simplest (and also, despite its bad track record in current statistics, still the most successful) form of mankind's dream of an ideal community in this world. A good marriage is the closest thing on earth to the realization of a practical, enduring, and loving coexistence between people. It is a sign, a spiritual and social and political example, of depths of love and patience and forgiveness that are unknown in other spheres of life. Every time a wedding takes place, the highest hopes and ideals of the whole community are rekindled. A wedding is the keynote address to the convention of human brotherhood. Not that anything like a perfect society will ever be possible in this world—yet still there is an instinctual sense that marriage leads the way, that universal peace can be conceived of only in terms of human beings coming together with something of the same spirit of love, unity, commitment, and self-sacrifice that are seen to operate at the heart of a good marriage. Marriage is the test case, the leading edge, and the *sine qua non* of love and brotherhood in the world.

For all these reasons, good marriages are the foundation of society. They are seeds, or cell groups, pointing the way to man's great dream of utopia, which is fundamentally his urgent longing for the kingdom of God. While the Church, of course, is the true harbinger of the kingdom, not even in the Church does the dedication of one particular human being to another turn out in practical terms to be so all-embracing, so fleshly, so deep and searing and permanent as in the lifelong eating-sleeping-thinking-together bond of marriage.

STANDING OR FALLING ON LOVE

While the world loves a wedding, on the whole its attitude toward marriage is one of ambivalence. Society senses the vast importance of marriage and therefore has made every effort to preserve and uphold it. But society also senses that marriage is a powerful weapon for the advancement of the kingdom of God, and that it stands for a depth of intimacy the world at large is decidedly suspicious and fearful of. The world is not set up for intimacy, but on the contrary for privacy, and for the most part it abhors the pain and honesty and humility that characterize deep human relationships.

As a result, society has bent over backwards not just to accommodate but also to tame, control, ritualize, belittle, mock, or otherwise drain marriage of its disturbing power, so that throughout history marriage as an institution has tended to become the pawn of selfish and worldly interests and to be subjugated to all manner of purposes other than the one it was intended for. There have been "arranged marriages," "good matches," and "marriages of convenience." Marriage has been considered the accepted thing, the socially prudent thing, and a valid means for improving status, comfort, economic security, power, and social connectedness. At the same time, the currency of marriage has been devalued through excessive romanticism, sexual exploitation, ersatz vows, the stalemate of common law, and recent efforts to legitimize same-sex liaisons. And throughout history the stereotyped roles of husband and wife have become the butt of a particularly callous brand of humor.

Nevertheless, in our own time it is curiously true that the integrity and vitality of marriage appear to be on the upswing. For in spite of the appalling decadence of Western culture, the importance of married intimacy is today being stressed and defended in a way that is perhaps unique in all of history. Never before has marriage been expected to produce such a high quality of interpersonal relationships. Never before have marriages been evaluated so single-mindedly by the sole criterion of love (which may be understood as the expressed desire for and promise of deep intimacy). In most circles today, marriage for any other reason than for love would be unthinkable, and by the same token being "out of love" is thought more widely than ever to be ample grounds for divorce.

So while countless marriages are falling apart, marriage itself thrives, taking on loftier aims and values, and many of the couples who do stay together are facing remarkable new challenges as they press on toward the very limits of personal encounter.

More and more as time goes on, it seems, marriage is being asked to stand alone, to be judged above and apart from all other considerations and practicalities, as a union of man and woman in which the single value of love transcends all others, and in which the achievement of intimacy is the sole yardstick of success. No other institution on earth (including, as we have seen, the church) has ever been subjected in a practical way to the enormous internal pressure of such agonizingly high ideals. There is nothing else in the world that humans recognize as standing or falling on the basis of pure loving intimacy. Other things continue, love or no love. But marriage without intimacy (although common enough in other periods of history) has come today to be almost a synonym for hell.

While this may seem to be a modern development, it is not a modern truth. For it has always been the case, in all times and cultures, that God's plan for marriage was that it should be a monogamous union based on love. If polygamy was permitted in Old Testament times, that is not to say God ever took pleasure in it for its own sake, any more than He took pleasure in the wars He Himself commanded the Israelites to fight. A distinction must be made between what God *wills* and what God *wants,* and within that perspective it becomes clear that polygamy in the Bible was never a divine ideal. For throughout Scripture it is always monogamous love, one-to-one intimacy, that is the soul of marriage, whether in the story of Eden (where Adam and Eve literally had no one else but one another), or in the example of Abraham (who was obviously closer to his first wife Sarah than he ever could be to

Hagar), or in the case of the polygamist King Rehoboam who, we are told, "loved Maacah daughter of Absalom more than any of his other wives and concubines" (2 Chronicles 11:21).

NOWHERE TO HIDE

If marriage today is under greater stress, and if contemporary couples are facing an entirely new order of problems, and if there are more breakdowns and separations and divorces than ever before, it is largely because the demand for intimacy in marriage has never been so overwhelming. Strangely enough, the very crisis in contemporary marriage is the surest indicator of its health as an ideal, and in the long run may function to bring the reality of marriage closer into line with the Lord's highest purposes for it. For modern marriage no longer has any leg to stand on apart from simple, naked love. That is its sole *raison d'être* today, that is all that can justify it, and it is more and more true that there is nowhere to hide in marriage, no way to escape its searing demands. Perhaps what is really happening in the process of history is that gradually it becomes clearer and clearer that not just any love can justify and bless a marriage, but only the love of Christ. For it is He who joins and keeps people together, not they themselves, nor any accident, nor any other power or persuasion under the sun. He is the Lord of marriage, and He holds the key to it. Surely this is the lesson the world is struggling to learn: that if you are not prepared in marriage to abandon yourself completely to love, and most especially to the love of God, then forget it! It may be that marriage in our day is turning out to be a much higher calling (and perhaps a much rarer one) than anyone ever supposed it to be.

And so the godless are fleeing from marriage in droves, and it is the most common thing in the world for modern men and women to have their lives regularly torn apart by the agony of one broken amorous union after another. Whatever security there may once have been in secular marriage is quickly being eroded. The decisive finality of vows was intended to free people so that they need not see their life's energies being drained away in endless courting rituals, in the constant hunger for sexual fulfillment, and in a continual search for meaningful relationships. But when marriage is discarded or devalued, how much time people begin to waste on their fickleness! Their talk is of nothing but relationships, and they never do find any real stability or lasting trust. Instead of growing into maturity with one partner, they go over and over the same basic ground in each new liaison. And through it all, heartbreak is the commonest of tragedies, far more common than bereavement. Indeed the heartbreak of a failed love relationship can actually be more distressing than bereavement and is perhaps the single most traumatic experience a human being can undergo. The grief that sets in after a separation tends to be much more prolonged and inconsolable than that following a death, if only because of the deliberateness of the abandonment, the repression of the normal grieving process, and the persistent fantasy of reunion.

It is no wonder that when Jesus instructed His disciples concerning divorce they concluded, "If this is the situation between a husband and wife, it is better not to marry" (Matthew 19:10). In our times we do not see obvious evidence that the Lord strikes people dead for their sin or commands whole nations to be put to the sword. But it is quite clear that the fabric of individual lives is being eaten away from the inside by the hunger for intimacy and the failure to attain it, and that the cup of the Lord's wrath is being poured out via the increasingly incorruptible vessel of matrimony. Even as more marriages than ever before are reduced to ashes, the union of matrimony itself emerges not only unscathed, but as a higher and a purer thing, more and more implacable in its holy demands, more unshakable than ever in the foundations of its sacred love. The biblical ideal of marriage cannot help but stand in judgment over contemporary society, laying wide open the sin and corruption of hearts, making woefully obvious the poverty of true intimacy in the world.

DISCOVERY AND DISCLOSURE

Marriage is to human relations what monotheism is to theology. It is a decision to put all the eggs in one basket, to go for broke, to bet all of the marbles. Is there any abandonment more pure, more supreme, more radically self-abnegating than that of putting one's entire faith in just one God, the Lord of all, in such a way as to allow that faith to have a searching impact on every corner of one's life? On the level of human relations, only one act of trust can begin to approach this one, and that is the decision to believe in one other person and to believe so robustly as to be ready to squander one's whole life on that one.

Consider the frightful power that marriage exercises over every aspect of a life, for joy or for trouble. It is estimated that only 5 percent of marriages are truly happy and fulfilling unions, while in most of the others the weight of disappointments, and the thought of the dreadful mistake that has been made, are carried around constantly like splinters in the heart. A bad marriage, as has been observed, can be the worst thing in the world, and perhaps the only thing worse yet is bad theology, a bad marriage with God. In either case the stakes are so horrifyingly high because what are at risk are the highest qualities of the human spirit: love, trust, faithfulness. In both marriage and faith it is the quality of devotion that is tested, the ability to give unwavering and undivided trust in one direction. For if we cannot trust one other person, neither can we trust ourselves; and if we cannot trust for a lifetime, then we cannot really trust at all. One single act of treason destroys a whole relationship, wiping out all the good that went before. Reconciliation is still possible, but only at the cost of total recommitment.

In the absence of a deep and abiding faith in the one Almighty Father, whose love is perfect, how inconstant will be the faith of an imperfect couple in one another! In this age of religious syncretism, surely the rareness of the former commitment has spelled disaster for the latter. Conversely, if we cannot be faithful to a living person we can see and touch, how will we ever be faithful to an invisible God? Human beings have not the capacity for any actions higher than those of enduring faith and love, and these qualities can only exist, let alone flourish, under conditions of unbroken intimacy. There can be no love, in other words, without enduring relationship, and the highest expression this can take is that of the covenant: the all-encompassing, voluntary, and unbreakable pact struck between two hearts.

Both Christianity and marriage are centrally concerned with the very depths of this covenant intimacy and therefore with the outer limits of personal encounter and exposure. A man may lose himself among many gods, but to accept the one true Lord is to allow himself to be found. Similarly in marriage the acceptance of one permanent partner turns out, in a profound way, to be an acceptance of oneself. For the closer we are drawn into the brilliant and mysterious circle of another person, the more must we ourselves be revealed in the other's light, revealed for what we are. Others are mirrors in which we are constrained to see ourselves, not as we would like to be, but as we are. Whenever we pull away, searching in one mirror after another for a more pleasing image, what we are really doing is avoiding the truth

What is hard about marriage is what is hard also about facing the Christian God: It is the strain of living continually in the light of a conscience other than our own, being under the intimate scrutiny of another pair of eyes. It is really judgment that we fear, the sense of being in the glare of a moral searchlight. That is what we shrink from, whether before God or in the presence of one another. It is what we thought we had escaped from when we left home, putting behind us the discipline of our parents and embracing the strange new freedom of adulthood, the sweet thrill of feeling absolutely unaccountable to anyone except ourselves. But marriage, we may soon find to our chagrin, has no respect for such independence, and neither does the God who is our true Father. Accountability is at the very heart of marriage, as of Christianity, and wherever else we may look in the world there can be no true intimacy without this ingredient of moral accountability. The only intimacy that is possible, and without which life is a horribly cold and lonely and hollow business, turns out to be a two-way channel involving both discovery and disclosure. We are insatiably curious to know all we can about others, to probe into the most secret details of their lives. But no such insight is possible until we ourselves submit to the humility of being known, which includes being known in all of our phoniness and pride, in all the frailty of our humanness and the blackness of our sin.

Who cares, really, to be known *that* well by another person? Who wishes to have the whole unexpurgated dossier of their lives opened up to such close surveillance? And yet that is the name of the game in marriage, where even the last vestiges of privacy are challenged—everything from the most secret of bedroom and toilet habits, to hypocrisies and falsehoods and the subtlest fluctuations of mood and thought. If a man has a pimple on his private parts, then his wife will know about it, and only his wife, and the same will be true of the minutest blemishes on his soul. For hiding is not what marriage is about. Marriage means being in the spotlight, being under the unceasing scrutiny of another person, just as we are all under the constant gaze of the Lord our God. Marriage is about nakedness, exposure, defenselessness, and the very extremities of intimacy. It is about simple unadorned truth between two human beings, truth at all levels and at all costs, and it does not care what pain or inconvenience must be endured in order for the habit of truth to take root, to be watered, and to grow into maturity. Marriage is a sacrament of openness, of personal knowledge, the supreme means provided by God for people to come to know one another. Only in decaying marriages is it true that anyone in the world (including parents, psychoanalyst, or confessor) knows us better than our spouse, or at the same time develops a deeper respect for all that is unknowable in us.

THE ARMOR OF WORTH

It is not intimacy itself, therefore, that is so distasteful and intimidating to the world but rather the moral condemnation that comes with it. People crave closeness with one another, but are repelled by the sin that such closeness inevitably uncovers in themselves: the selfish motives that are unmasked, the pettiness that spills out, the monstrous new image of self that emerges as it struggles so pitifully to have its own way.

Of course, only God can give people the strange desire to know the whole truth about themselves, and the strength and courage to live wide-open, exposed lives before one another. And how does He do it? How does He slip us this bitter pill, coated with intense desire and determination? Fortunately, the pill is also lavishly coated with the mystery we call love, which is the only thing in heaven or on earth that can shield us from the horror of knowing what we are really like. That, in fact, is what God's love is: It is His armor, an armor of forgiveness and acceptance that we put on over our corruption, an armor of worth or worthiness that completely covers our own worthlessness. God's love is, in a sense, the courage to go on living in the face of our sin, in the full knowledge of who and what we are. This intolerable knowledge of self must, indeed, be exchanged for knowledge of the Lord, and supremely for the knowledge of His saving power through the love of His Son Jesus Christ. That is what it means to "put on" Christ: It is to assume His strength and purity and goodness, recognizing that we have none of our own. Such an actual transfusion of character is possible only in the depths of loving intimacy with God in Christ.

And so it is in marriage that when the Lord draws a man and a woman together in the most intimate of human associations, He does so by giving them His love, which is all that can shield them through the searing experience of self-revelation they are to undergo. This is an experience that all people both crave and fear, with a fear that is conquerable only by love. Only love can drive out the constant threat of condemnation and rejection that otherwise haunts and spoils all experiences of intimacy. People cannot seem to refrain from judging one another, and in the crucible of marriage the judgment can be so intense and oppressive that the only recourse is a loving forgiveness of the other's wrongs, and in turn a courageous willingness to see one's own sinfulness exposed, conquered, and actually replaced by the other's love. In such a relationship, a true transfusion and transformation of characters may take place as each puts on the good qualities of the other and forgives the bad. Each is armor to the other, each is the other's strength and worth.

The process of discovering or finding another person is the process of losing oneself. This is certainly not a loss of identity, but only of the false identity that is founded upon self-will. Human beings are the presence of God in the world, and by drawing so close to one of them that we enter willingly into the fire of his or her judgment, it becomes possible for our own selfish will to be illuminated and cauterized. Intimacy is thus a fire of righteous purification, a fire we could never tolerate were it not for the assurance that we are loved. Such assurance cannot be bought except at the price of the only thing we have to give, which is our faithfulness, the dedication of our whole hearts to another.

We must buy others, in a sense, at the cost of ourselves, at the expense of painful self-disclosure and annihilation, just as Jesus bought us through the agonizing and passionate disclosure of the depths of God's love in the sacrifice of His own body on the cross.

HAVING AND HOLDING

When we have bought another person with our whole hearts, we may naturally and truly be said to possess them. Modern couples balk at this idea, and possessiveness in marriage has come to be regarded as a cardinal sin. But there is no true marriage without it, and even in the vows there is embedded that curious and potent little phrase "to have and to hold." As Paul says, "The wife's body does not belong to her alone but also to her husband. In the same way, the husband's body does not belong to him alone but also to his wife" (1 Corinthians 7:4). Ownership is expressed in this passage in terms of sexual rights, just as property owners have certain exclusive rights over their land. But the physical is always a sign of something deeper, and in marriage not just the body is given, but the heart. One heart is given in exchange for another, and in this mutual proprietorship is found the deepest and most radical expression of intimacy. It might almost be said that love is the total willingness to be owned.

Granted, ownership by a mere human being is hard to submit to, difficult even to conceive of. But that is why it requires the highly specialized conditions of matrimony. Marriage creates the only circumstance under which one person may rightfully be said to possess another. Such ownership is intended, of course, to reflect God's ownership of His creatures. In allowing another person rights of proprietorship over us, we learn something of what it means to be possessed by the Lord, to have no hesitation in giving ourselves to Him, because He owns us already.

Does this mean that God can be accused of possessiveness? Of course! St. Augustine, in one of the most probing and beautiful sentences in all of literature, prays to the Lord at the beginning of his *Confessions*, "You made us for Yourself, and our hearts find no peace until they rest in You." There is really no escaping it: God has made us for Himself, He has full rights to us, we are His possessions. The Lord has many names, and one of them is Jealous: "Do not worship any other god, for the LORD, whose name is Jealous, is a jealous God" (Exodus 34:14). Does He not burn with jealousy when we try to renounce His claim on us, giving ourselves to other masters? What sort of love would it be if our Maker looked on tolerantly and dispassionately as we destroyed ourselves, cutting ourselves off from our own life? For the Lord knows that He Himself is our Life, and His jealous possessiveness of us is thus an expression of the greatest possible concern for our well-being.

There is a jealousy, then, a righteous jealousy, that far from being incommensurate with love is inherent in it. And since love is love, what is true of divine love is true also (or ought to be) of human love. There is a place for jealousy in marriage, as each partner, knowing instinctively that the other cannot possibly find any rest or satisfaction outside of complete loyalty, seeks jealously to secure and to safeguard the other's faithfulness, and therefore the other's peace. Just as they are both the Lord's possessions (and He is theirs, too!), so also must a husband and wife recognize that they belong to one another. In fact this very sense of belonging was their reason for getting married in the first place. More than a belonging *with,* it is a belonging *to;* more than being completed, it is being possessed.

The world knows no greater power than that which is unleashed when one human being becomes the property of another. That, in fact, is exactly what the world means by power: It means the control, the authority, the proprietary influence of one person or group over others. That is what wars, government, and money are all about. But the power that the world tries to grab for itself is nothing at all beside the intimate dominion of one life over another bestowed freely by God in love. Love is the only true power, because it is the only thing that does not want power, just as love is the only true wealth because it is the only thing that can afford to give itself away.

The very heart of intimacy is reached when two people are neither afraid nor ashamed of being possessed by love, when in fact they give themselves freely to the pure joy and liberty of owning and being owned. There is a delicious relaxation, an unspeakable peace in knowing that one belongs in another's arms, and that far from being swallowed up by the other's heart, it is there that the mystery of one's own true identity opens up as never before. For our identity is hidden in love, in a love that cannot exist at all until it gives itself away. A robust spirit of abandonment, but equally of possessiveness, is one more of the ways a marriage may reflect the very attributes of God.

When Joseph was resisting the overtures of Potiphar's wife, he told her, "Everything my master owns he has entrusted to my care…. He has withheld nothing from me except you, because you are his wife" (Genesis 39:8–9). He recognized that a spouse is a possession, but a possession like no other, the most personal of all effects, one that is like one's very own life in that it cannot possibly be given to anyone else. For marriage is the grafting together of two hearts, the planting of them in one another so that they become interdependent for their very life. It is intended to be a picture of the way we all belong to Jesus, as branches to the vine.

This is not to claim, of course, that a husband and wife own one another outright, entirely, as they are owned by the Lord. But in truth they do own one another more than they can be said to own anything else in the whole world. When a husband looks with love into the eyes of his wife, he may know beyond a shadow of doubt that those eyes, and the person within them, belong to him, in a way that nothing else on earth can—neither his house, nor his car, nor his insurance policy, nor his children, nor any other person. She is his, to have and to hold, for life.

So radical is the extremity of this mutual ownership in marriage, and so complete is the symbiosis, that only death can sever it, as only love can confer it. The very experience of falling in love, indeed, is that of God giving one person to another. Only He can do that. Only God can give people away.

FOUR

love is a choice

Vows

He who loves his wife loves himself.

— EPHESIANS 5.28

Vows

IMPOSSIBLE PROMISES

A marriage is not a joining of two worlds, but an abandoning of two worlds in order that one new one might be formed.

In this sense, the call to be married bears comparison with Jesus' advice to the rich young man to sell all his possessions and to follow Him. It is a vocation to total abandonment. For most people, in fact, marriage is the single most wholehearted step they will ever take toward a fulfillment of Jesus' command to love one's neighbor as oneself. For every marriage partner begins as a neighbor, and often enough a neighbor who has been left beaten and wounded on the road of love, whom all the rest of the world has in a sense passed by. What a strange impulse it is that moves us to appreciate the tremendous value of this particular person in a way no other stranger ever has, to the point of committing ourselves totally to them in love, even unto death!

Such a step, of course, cannot be taken or even contemplated without the enabling grace and love of God. Naturally many marriages are undertaken, and even last, without any conscious or volitional recourse to God's help, or without any dependence upon

Him whatsoever. But there are no lasting marriages without the continuing secret touch of His grace, which comes to a couple in the form of the uncanny ability to keep a set of highly improbable promises to one another, promises involving such normally evanescent qualities as love, honor, trust, faithfulness. How can anyone ever bring himself to affirm that he will care for another person twenty years from now? It is one thing to promise your girlfriend that you will pick her up at eight o'clock; it is quite another to give her your pledge that you will love her for the rest of your life. The marriage vows are simple ones, but remarkable for the extremity of their loftiness, for the foolhardiness of their altruism, and further remarkable for the fact that in most cases they turn out to be the only true vows either partner will ever make, let alone hold to, in their entire lives. So remarkable are these foolish little promises that after just one year of them (to say nothing of twenty or fifty!) a couple will be left shaking their heads in bewilderment and wonder, amazed that they have kept their word, hardly believing what they know to be true.

Yet equally will there be complete astonishment and devastation if the promises should ever come to be broken. For in a very real way these are not the couple's promises at all, but the Lord's. In purely human terms the marriage vows are impossible: impossible to keep, and impossible to walk away from. Only the very naive get married under the delusion that they will have an easy time of it. But most rational adults approach marriage in the full knowledge that they have no idea what they are doing. Whatever god they believe in, it is all in his hands, and even for the irreligious a wedding, like a deathbed, will normally be felt as a serious enough occasion to inspire a secret prayer.

For the Christian, however, there is a certain comfort in the fact that there are few more unlikely institutions than marriage, and few steps that turn out to be more radical in their long-term implications, and that all in all the task is such an incredibly tall order that it could have been set and invented only by God and can be carried out with any real success only by means of His infinite mercy and love, through an utter abandonment to His will every step of the way.

A Kept Man and Woman

Holy matrimony represents the most popular set of religious vows in history. So popular are these vows that most people in modern times do not even think of them as vows at all, but simply as a sort of glorified folk custom, one of life's little rituals that it's probably better to go along with than not. One says the vows the way one swears on the Bible in court. If there is anything awe-inspiring about the procedure, it has more to do with the sobering thought of its binding legality and the emotion of the moment than it has with anything supernatural.

But make no mistake about it: The joining of a man and a woman in matrimony is a supernatural event, founded upon a mutual exchange of holy pledges. As we have seen, these pledges are the only true vows that most people will ever take. They may even be the only truly sacred words that ever escape a couple's mouths. The saying of them requires about thirty seconds. But keeping them is the work of a lifetime.

To keep a vow, however, does not mean to keep from breaking it. If that were the case, marriage vows would be broken the day they were made. This is where a vow differs from a mere promise or resolution. A resolution, once broken, must either be forgotten or made again. But a vow retains its power and validity irrespective of conduct. It is not like the signing of a legal contract and not like any other form of human promise. A person cannot promise to love another person; he can only vow to do so. A vow is, per se, a confession of inadequacy and an automatic calling upon the only adequacy there is, which is the mercy and power of God.

To keep a vow, therefore, means not to keep from breaking it, but rather to devote the rest of one's life to discovering what the vow means, and to be willing to change and to grow accordingly. It might almost be said that the sign of a vow being kept is the realization of how far one is from keeping it. In a very real way, the vow keeps the man rather than vice versa. A vow may keep a man honest, for example, by facing him day in and day out with the depth of his insincerity, and he may be kept loving through a continual confrontation with his own unloveliness. The vow is a mystery, an insoluble riddle, that somehow corrects and shames him at the same time it picks him up and spurs him on to higher things. So a married person is a kept person, kept in the profound protection of vows that have been taken before the Lord. This is not the protection of a lazy security and comfort; rather, it is the protection of an inexhaustible forgiveness.

How Dark a Night?

Most people assume that what holds a marriage together is the couple's love for one another. But of course it is not. For where is love when the divorce proceedings begin? All that remains at that point, as the final obstacle or knot to be untied, are the vows, and the undoing of these vows is no mere formality. It may be a formality in a court of law, before human witnesses, but in the eyes of God and in the practical experience of the couple, it will not be a formality. There are no mere formalities in matters of the heart.

So while love must certainly be present if a marriage is to continue and be successful, practically speaking (and the practical level is always the deepest and most mystical) the vows really hold the thing together, undergirding love itself. Of course, this is just another way of saying that love is not an emotion or an experience but a promise, a resolve, an act of the will. The impact of love may be felt as an exclamation mark, but vows ask a question. "How bright is the sun!" exclaims love, while the vows ask, "How dark a night are you prepared to pass through?" Marriages that are dependent on good feelings fall apart, or at best are in for a stormy time of it. But marriages that consistently look back to their vows, to those wild promises made before God, and that trust Him to make sense out of them, find a continual source of strength and renewal.

One very important fact to know in marriage is that there is always a way out. And the way out is not divorce. No, the way out in marriage (no matter how bad things may get) is simply to put everything we have back on the line, our whole hearts and lives, just as we did the moment we took our vows. We must return to an attitude of total abandonment, of throwing all our natural caution and defensiveness to the winds and putting ourselves entirely in the hands of love by an act of the will. Instead of falling into love, we may now have to march into it.

There is an old bit of wise and practical marital advice, often quoted, suggesting that couples who begin to feel themselves "out of love" should return to doing the sort of things they did together when they *were* in love, even if it means sitting whole summer evenings side by side on the porch swing, with no other entertainment but one another. Originally we did these things only with the help of God's gift of an enormous groundswell of fervent motivation and natural attraction in our hearts. But God is not interested, ultimately, in natural attraction. He wants us to come to know the supernatural attraction of His own sort of love. So later in life, we may be called upon to repeat in marriage our original acts of love and abandonment, but this time without much help from the emotions, and without any help at all from romantic love. We may be called upon to act all alone, out of pure faith and trust, perhaps without even the perceived help of our partner. For it is often God's way that what He Himself has taught us to do in the light, we must repeat on our own in the darkness.

We needn't think of this as surrendering to our mate, necessarily, but rather as giving in to marriage itself and obeying the only two firm instructions the New Testament gives concerning marriage: that it be a union of love, and that there be no divorce (two commandments that, incidentally, need to be given about equal weight, so that there is little sense obeying the latter while neglecting the former). For marriage, sanctified as it is by God's promise of love, is that big a thing that it is quite worthy of a wholehearted surrender to it, no matter what sort of a sinner our partner may have become. When we surrender to marriage and to the sinner God once unaccountably gave us the ability to love, then we surrender in faith and in the very depth of our will to God Himself. This is the sort of act that will be required of us in eternity, once all the surface bustle of our earthly lives is past. We must learn here and now to see the invisible and to do the impossible.

CHOOSING ETERNITY

We ourselves cannot make a promise that we will not be fickle; only God can do that. Only God can promise protection from the changefulness and decadence of our own desperately fickle hearts, and in doing so He gives us a glimpse into the meaning of eternal life. Marriage is one of the supreme earthly ways by which God enables men and women to choose eternity, and actually to grow into His own changelessness and constancy by slowly acquiring the only constancy that is possible in this world of decay, which is the constancy of the heart, the constancy of loving faithfulness. By letting the Lord teach us through marriage how to withdraw from all temptation to change partners, to love another, to be single again, to harden our hearts, or to let our love grow cold, we begin here and now to taste and to participate in the qualities of eternity. This is possible only through a deliberate claiming of the Lord's promises in the form of a vow.

The taking of vows is an act of faith. If people were faithful by nature, vows would not be necessary; their yes would be yes and their no would be no. But it is because people are not inherently faithful nor honest nor loving that they must stand up and declare they will be. The public declaration does not automatically transform them into marvelous creatures of virtue who will always keep to their word. On the contrary, it only makes more obvious and public their complete lack of personal virtue, calling upon the witness and support of the whole community of their friends and relatives and emphasizing their dependence upon resources that are utterly beyond human strength.

The marriage vows give glory to God. While it is true that a man and a woman on their wedding day take a step toward a unique fulfillment of the commandment of love, it is even more true to say of matrimony that it is a sacramental outpouring of God's grace enabling such love to take place. The human couple indicates humbly a willingness to give themselves to this love; but it is the Lord who makes love possible in the first place, and therefore He promises that His gift of love will not be taken away.

Therefore, anyone who has taken these vows (assuming they have been taken in good faith) need no longer worry about falling out of love. For we have vowed not to. Nor will there be any justification for anxiety over the possibility of our loved one getting fat, ugly, sick, old, being unable to work anymore, or doing something evil or shameful. For we have vowed to continue loving in spite of all changes and adversity, in spite of good times, bad times, wealth, or poverty. In making such reckless promises we have freely admitted that we ourselves cannot keep them, yet equally freely have we confessed our unreserved faith in and dependence upon the God who can, the God whose very nature is expressed in faithfulness, that is, in the keeping of apparently impossible promises to His people.

A church wedding makes it very clear that there is no security whatsoever in human passion and resolve, but only in the Lord's passion and the Lord's resolve. The wedding is a ceremonial declaration that God has brought two people together, and that He has already taken it upon Himself to keep them together. It is not any human power that has joined them, any more than a human power may "put them asunder" (Matthew 19:6). The wedding is an acceptance and proclamation of God's power to take action of eternal significance in the lives of mortals, to step in and overrule the fickleness of the human heart. It is not that the vows hold any guarantee that a couple shall always be *in* love, but rather that through God's grace and strength they may continue in faith *to* love. For that, once again, is the peculiar meaning of Christian love: not a feeling, but an action, and not a human and limited action, but a supernatural and eternal one. Love is a deep, continuous, growing, and ever-renewing activity of the will, superintended by the Holy Spirit. There is no question of its failing or ceasing or letting anyone down. A wedding, therefore, declares openly and robustly that there is nothing romantic about love, nothing the least bit chancy or changeable. It is a gift from the Lord, whole and intact forever, a sure rock.

Naturally those who stubbornly refuse to believe this will fail to experience the reality of it. For them the marriage vows will be at best a polite and suitable agreement, at worst a bad taste in the mouth, a twisting knife in the heart, so much dust sifting tragically and inexplicably through wrinkling, stiffening fingers.

EXTRAVAGANT SIMPLICITY

The problem with most troubled marriages is that both partners are trying to accomplish far too many things in the world, and in the process, like Martha in Luke 10:42, they neglect the "one thing needful." Next to the love of God, the one thing by far the most important in the life of all married people is their marriage, their loving devotion to their partner. Nothing on earth must take precedence over that, not children, jobs, other friendships, nor even "Christian work."

As obvious as it sounds, this can be a most difficult priority to keep in perspective. For what it amounts to, finally, is that it is not just the bad and the selfish in oneself that must be continually renounced if one is to be successfully married. Even more painful and bewildering to cope with are all the good and healthy things that must be renounced or postponed or watered down on account of the demands imposed by marriage. How many deep friendships that might have been are rendered impractical by marriage, or must at least take a backseat to the primary friendship with one's spouse? How many wonderful activities are interrupted by marriage duties, and how many good intentions and charitable plans must be set aside each day? How much energy that might otherwise have been put at the service of the church or the community is channeled instead into the work of marriage? Like Judas Iscariot at the sight of Mary pouring out costly perfume over the feet of Jesus, we cry out, "This ointment might have been sold, and the money given to the poor!" (John 12:5). What offends us is the terrible waste of marriage, the waste of our precious lives being poured out over just one other person. We would like to think of ourselves, perhaps, as having a great impact on the world, touching and influencing thousands of lives. How great is our frustration when we realize that we do not adequately touch even the one single life of the person closest to us!

However, part of the secret to the effectiveness and strength of the peculiar little vows of marriage lies in this very scandal of waste, this extravagant simplicity of focus. For marriage involves nothing more than a lifelong commitment to love just one person—to do, whatever else one does, a good, thorough job of loving one person. What could be simpler than that? There is nothing simpler than love.

Granted, the simplest thing of all is to love the Lord God, and loving a person is a little more complicated than that. But that is where the marriage vows come in: Their purpose is effectively to remove all the complications that people normally put in the way of loving one another, so as to reduce love to its simplest and most potent terms. While the rest of the world runs after grandiose and unattainable ideals, married partners walk the humbler but more accessible path of simple caring for one another from one day to the next. It is a task that is not very glorious from the point of view of the world, but one that could hardly be more important in the eyes of God. And there is no greater peace or fulfillment than in doing a few simple things for the love of God, the things He Himself has put closest to hand.

When couples observe (as they are fond of doing) that marriage requires work, what they mean primarily is that it takes time.

They mean it robs them of precious time. They mean that marriage gobbles up unbelievable enormities, scandalous vastnesses, great fantastic globs and scads of pure, priceless, unrecoverable time. It is like the amount of fuel that must be fed into a big, powerful, shiny, eight-cylinder gas guzzler that has to be kept constantly on the road. You cannot leave a marriage sitting in the driveway even for a day, because the only reason for marriage is togetherness. It is an alliance of love, and love is a spiritual vehicle, a rocket ship, that travels faster and farther than anything else under the sun. Get out of it for a moment, and it leaves without you for parts unknown; let it idle, and it begins to rust; neglect it, and it falls apart. It can be a full-time job just being a passenger in this thing. But like it or not, you and your spouse are in it together, and in it for life, and the work of traveling in marriage is the most vital work you can do. In the Lord's plans for the world there is no work more important than the work of relationship, and no relationship is more important than one's marriage.

For marriage inevitably becomes the flagship of all other relationships. One's own home is the place where love must first be practiced before it can truly be practiced anywhere else. No one likes to be out of joint with a good friend or with in-laws or with an employer, but such problems at least can be tolerated. Yet any little thing that comes between a man and his wife is capable of wrenching them apart inside, and if that is not the case, then it can only be due to the growth of a callousness in them that cannot help carrying over into all their other relationships. A husband and wife are "one flesh," and to be alienated from one another is equivalent to being alienated from their own bodies. How can a man who harbors bitterness toward himself be anything but bitter toward the rest of the world? "He who loves his wife loves himself," says Paul (Ephesians 5:28). That is how closely God has bound a couple together in Christ. He has ordained that charity, which is Christian love, begin at home.

This is what a radical business these little vows of marriage involve us in: They pit the needs and wants of one small, frail, love-starved human creature against the demands of all the rest of the universe, with all of its urgency and glory and importance, and there is no contest! It is our spouse who must win. It is the one person who wins over the many, the humble cause of the home that prevails over every other worthy cause in the world. While it is true that Jesus declared, "If anyone comes to me and does not hate his wife...he cannot be my disciple" (Luke 14:26), He might have gone on to say with equal astringency that no one can love a wife without first hating all other people. It is not hatred that is the point, of course, but rather the order of priorities in the heart. As the vows taken at baptism acknowledge the Lord Jesus to hold the position of absolute preeminence in a person's life, so the vows of marriage establish each partner in a human relationship that takes unquestionable priority over all other ties. The vows make it possible for any ordinary person to begin to become as fully and overwhelmingly important in the life of just one other human being as each one of us is, mysteriously, in the life of God.

Love with a Focus

This is not to say that marriage is a narrow, inward-looking clique, a mutual admiration society of two in which each member must expend all available energy in the love of just one person. On the contrary, any marriage that does not recognize its vows as not simply a commitment to one other person, but to all the rest of humanity, is not a marriage worthy of the name. At its most fundamental level, marriage is a union between *self* and *other*, and not just with one other, but with all others: with everything that is *other*, everything that is *not self*. One recognizes the impossibility of carrying out such a union in any practical terms on earth, yet nevertheless expresses a willingness to do just that, an openness to that ultimate aim, and makes a practical beginning in marriage. One does one's utmost to be wholly united to just one other person and thereby admits one's limitations, yet at the same time takes it on faith that a beginning has to be made somewhere, that such a wholehearted commitment has to and *can* be made somewhere, and that far from being purely symbolic, such an act will in fact render one better able, in practice, to be united in love to all others.

For love is not like a river, confined between two banks. Its very essence is to overflow. But a river that is only half-full cannot overflow, let alone one that is dried up. So the point is not that the exercise of love is so taxing and time-consuming that it must be limited to our homes. On the contrary, the vow of love to one special person is intended to fill us up to the brim with love, to train us in the very depths of love and so to *free* us to have much more love for others than ever before. For it is not really the love in a home that eats up time and energy but rather the lack of love. That is what really wreaks havoc in our married life, ensnaring us in never-ending self-analysis and robbing us of the energy to love others.

In taking marriage vows, we are doing what the Lord Himself did with Abraham: making a promise of love to one individual. In keeping this promise, we are actually mirroring the Lord's own faithfulness to all His people, a faithfulness designed from the beginning to spill over to the whole of mankind. Why was it, in the great history of salvation, that the Lord Himself chose to concentrate His efforts on the special covenanted love of one chosen people, declaring to them that "you of all the nations shall be my very own" (Exodus 19:5)? Was it because God had only enough love to spare for one small group of people? Far from it! Rather, it was because love is only love when it is particular, and when the person receiving it is the object of special extremities of attention. Even Jesus hesitated to help a Canaanite woman, saying, "I was sent only to the lost sheep of Israel" (Matthew 15:24). But it was precisely because His ministry was to a select group that it became capable of spilling over into the whole world. There was nothing vague or hazily defined about Jesus' love. It was not the sort of mushy, universalist sentiment that claims in theory to love everyone but in practice loves no one. No, Jesus' love had a practical focus, and for that very reason it was able to overflow to all those outside that immediate focus. It was a focus trained not only on the people of Israel but more especially on one small ragged band of those people, and indeed even on one particular person within that small group, "the disciple whom Jesus loved."

Although Jesus Himself never married, His strategy of concentrated love nevertheless provides the pattern for couples and reveals God's own strategy, His inmost intentions for the marriage unit. Clearly He has planned, through marriage, for the demands of love to be made so concrete, so immediate and particular, so focused and intense as to become inescapable. It is His way of turning love into a do-or-die situation. As we saw earlier, marriage inevitably is a trap, a very cunning trap in which two people are caught in the absolute necessity of loving one another. In the taking of vows, it is as if they have agreed to an actual ultimatum: love or else. This is a curious and frustrating and often excruciatingly painful trap to be in, but the plain fact is that if a couple do not love one another first, as they do themselves, then they cannot really love themselves or anyone else. But when they do love, that love becomes a fire that has the power to enkindle all around them.

COVENANT FAITHFULNESS

The meaning of the marriage vows finds its deepest resonance, then, in the biblical concept of covenant, in which two parties so bind themselves to one another that the simple maintenance of their relationship becomes the most important and central thing in all of life, the basis from which everything else flows. Adherence to the vows is not a confining but a delimiting discipline, a marking of the natural boundaries of our human abilities. Far from being trapped, we are actually set free, set free and consecrated to perform a task that turns out to be the most vital work in the world: the work of covenant, of loving relationship. This may appear to us to be very obscure work, work we ourselves might not ever have made room for in our busy schedules. But nonetheless it is work the Lord views as important, so important that He has actually designed the whole of life with the specific intention of sharing with us the joy of it.

So central and momentous is this relational work of marriage that if a person who is called to it fails to perform it well, then all his other work, no matter how good it might be, will be called into question. Who wants to go to a divorced psychiatrist? Who will trust what a politician says about peace if there is not peace in his own home? Who wants to listen to a preacher who has a rotten marriage? One obvious biblical exception, of course, was the prophet Hosea, whose beleaguered marriage became the very kernel of his prophecy. But Hosea himself was faithful to his adulterous wife, and the corruption in his marriage reflected that of the whole society, and specifically the corruption at the heart of Israel's worship. Once again, we see marriage as the most intimate barometer of spiritual life: Alienation within marriage is symptomatic of the deepest alienation of all, that of a people from themselves and from their God, while married love is held up as the image of God's own love and faithfulness. At the same time, we learn from Hosea that what the Lord expects of a marriage is not always that it be happy and successful. What He wants is not success, but primarily that deep inner quality of faithfulness that, in its capacity to rise above all vicissitudes and all appearances of failure, is a reflection of the Lord's faithfulness toward a wayward people.

That is how we must love one another, with a vowed love that is not dependent upon happiness nor any of the external hallmarks of success. Where is such love to begin if it does not begin with the one nearest us, the life's partner we ourselves have chosen out of all the other people in the world as the apple of our eye? If we cannot love our own favorite person through all of his ups and downs and trials and changes, then how will we ever love the poor and the unlovely and the forgotten of the world? God has a way of giving us one love that is greater than all the others we know or have ever known, one love that is entirely easy (at least in the beginning) to fulfill, a natural and spontaneous love such as the one Jesus Himself seems to have had for John. For in these natural loves it is as if God is saying to us, "See how simple love is, how full of joy and freedom! Now take this gift as your model. Preserve and cherish it, and use it as a light to illumine all your other relationships. For I want to prove to you the potential of love and to teach you to love as I do, unconditionally, that you may share abundantly in My own life."

When we stop to think about it, it is a far stranger thing for people to love than not to, and stranger still for one person to be faithful in love to one other for a lifetime, than for people to be constantly changing loyalties. The latter is simply the commoner and more expected thing, which is to say that an enduring marriage is a living, breathing miracle. It is plain proof that love can actually exist in this loveless world and not only exist but persist and grow through all the chances and changes of life. If two people can love, then love is alive, more than it is in all the dreams of a utopian society or in all the peace resolutions of all the world's governments and organizations. A loving marriage is a solid guarantee that no matter what else may happen, at least there will be some love in the world.

Marriage or Celibacy?

If all of this is true, and if marriage really is the purest and at the same time the most practical worldly metaphor of the Lord's own covenant love, then why is it that the New Testament appears to advise against marriage? Why, in fact, is marriage portrayed even as a disadvantage for the Christian, as a worldly duty that cannot help detracting from wholehearted devotion to God? A book on Christian marriage can hardly escape dealing with this issue, particularly as it is outlined by Paul in a puzzling section of his first letter to the Corinthians. For on the one hand Paul says, "It is good for a man not to marry," but on the other hand, "It is better to marry than to burn with passion." And he goes on: "Those who marry will face many troubles in this life, and I want to spare you this…. I would like you to be free from concern"; and in conclusion, "He who marries the virgin does right, but he who does not marry her does even better" (1 Corinthians 7:1, 9, 28, 32, 38). What is Paul talking about here? Why does the beautiful bond of marriage come off as second-best to celibacy and even as a sort of steam valve for lust?

Sometimes in interpreting Scripture, it can be important to consider not so much what the author was trying to say (as much as that is supposed to be the cornerstone of all good exegesis), but rather what *effect* his words are likely to have on the reader. And what is the effect of Paul's extremely cautious advice concerning marriage? Well, certainly it has been the occasion for much guilt and coldness of feet in many a Christian romance, for many broken engagements, for many vows of celibacy. But even more to the point, it has occasioned an enormous amount of soul-searching: that process of deep and painful questioning into the very well-springs of one's motives, intentions, and expectations and into the mind and pleasure of the Lord. One cannot take this passage in Corinthians seriously, and at the same time seriously consider getting married, without the agonizing wheels of such a process being set in motion. This chapter is a stumbling block, and always has been, for those desiring and daring to get married. It puts the brakes on and in a most perplexing fashion. For anyone who has ever actually faced head-on the question of whether or not God wants him to marry knows perfectly well that Paul's advice to the Corinthians offers not one particle of real help or comfort in such a situation. If anything, it confuses and complicates the issue more than ever.

But therein, precisely, lie the power and effectiveness of these words. For was not Jesus Himself a stumbling block, a completely unexpected wrench thrown into the works of salvation, whose very presence serves to complicate and confuse all the central issues of life long before anything is ever clarified? And if we examine His teaching method, certainly He was concerned (more than Paul was) not just to give advice but to withhold it. His way was not always to provide answers, but more often simply to create a climate of moral and theological questioning such that the true searcher could himself hit upon the right answer. For that is the essence of the gospel teaching: not the laying down of laws but the opening up of the believer's heart so that he himself might discover the law that is already written there.

Few Christians, in short, have gone ahead with marriage on the strength of Paul's advice to the Corinthians. It is not a passage that is read at weddings! Many have gotten married in spite of it, in ignorance, skepticism, complete befuddlement, or even in frank defiance. But just because of this, perhaps it illustrates an important point of tension between Christians and their Scripture: For contrary to the assumption of many, Scripture was not given to be obeyed; rather, it was given that the Lord might be obeyed. The error of the Pharisees, after all, was that in seeking to obey Scripture to the letter, they actually neglected the true love and service of God. Certainly the same can be said about many Christian sects, who have abused the letter of the New Testament just as the Pharisees abused the Law. For the law of the Lord, ironically, turns out to be not merely a law but a charter: a proclamation of rights and freedoms and privileges.

What freedom is it that Scripture proclaims in these words of Paul to the Corinthians? Obviously, what is proclaimed is the complete freedom of the Christian to make up his own mind whether or not to be married. And this is done in such a way that the one who chooses marriage over celibacy makes a choice that is in fact far freer, and much more carefully considered and deeply thought out, than it ever could have been without Paul's warnings. There is a way in which Paul actually *abandons* his readers to the terrible existential reality of their own Christian freedom. He forces them into a corner in which a decision to get married can only be an absolutely radical one, a daring and unconventional exercise of God-given choice. In that way he recognizes the true character of the marriage vows as a most amazing and audacious adventure indeed, and at the same time rescues marriage from the stale and lifeless institution into which the secular world has always tended to mold it. It is not that Paul demeans marriage; rather, he turns it into a truly Christian option. Paul *saves* marriage for Christianity, even as he saves and sanctifies the alternative option of celibacy.

FIVE

the healing of shame

Sex

*The man and his wife were both
naked, and they felt no shame.*

—GENESIS 2:25

Sex

IMAGE AND INCARNATION

I sometimes wonder what it is like for nudists, whether they ever really get used to it. As for me, I still haven't gotten used to seeing my own wife naked. It's almost as if her body is shining with a bright light, too bright to look at for very long. I cannot take my eyes off her—and yet I must. To gaze too long or too curiously is, even with her, a breach of propriety, almost a crime. It is not like watching a flower or creeping up to spy on an animal in the wild. No, my wife's body is brighter and more fascinating than a flower, shier than any animal, and more breathtaking than a thousand sunsets. To me her body is the most awesome thing in creation. Trying to look at her, just trying to take in her wild, glorious beauty, so free and primal, so utterly unchanged since the beginning of time (despite what the evolutionists may think), I catch a small glimpse of what it means that men and women have been made in the image of God. If even the image is this dazzling, what must the Original be like?

In marriage we learn that nakedness, like God Himself, is inexhaustibly contemplable. We can never really see it, never quite look directly at it, for at one and the same time it is both a revelation and a darkness, a shining and a secret. That shy but driving curiosity we have about other human bodies will be with us all our lives. There is a Peeping Tom in all of us, for we can never see enough, never drink our fill. The truth of this is grossly mirrored in the man who is a slave of lust, for whom one stripper or one glossy photograph is never enough. But such lust of the eyes and of the flesh is only the perversion of a perfectly natural and healthy curiosity, healthy because it is the Lord Himself who has made us curious, who has caused us to be fascinated with one another's flesh. God has given the naked body its shining glory and has done so for the sole purpose of making it a marvelous harbinger of His own infinitely more lustrous glory.

But there is another aspect to the wonder of flesh, another facet of its glory, and that is the Incarnation. For not only have human beings been made in *imago Dei,* like unto God, but He also has not been ashamed to become one of us, to be incarnate in *imago homini.* Even our rude skin-and-bones image of God is hallowed, the Lord having graced it with His own indwelling, and the human body is an infinitely more sacred thing since God Himself has been in it. No matter how deformed or unsightly our body may be, in the blazing light of the Incarnation it is revealed, simply by association with the Lord Jesus, to be holier than anything else in the material universe—as holy a thing, indeed, as the elements of the Eucharist. For the Communion bread is the body of Christ, but so are we who believe in Him. He lives in us by faith.

Some spark of God, it is true, may be said to inhere in the sun and in trees and in the tiniest bacteria, but He Himself does not *live* in these things and never has. He is not a god who would suddenly cease to exist if the whole material creation were to collapse, blow up, or vanish overnight, for He is the One who made it; He was here before it was. He is in every way a transcendent God, utterly distinct from His creation, present everywhere yet residing nowhere but in Himself, which is to say in Heaven, in Christ, in the Holy Spirit, and, by an astounding gift of grace, in His people. Only with the coming of Jesus Christ into the world did the total immaculateness of the divine being become fully present in material form, uncompromisingly incarnate. When the Creator visited His creation to dwell in it bodily, it was not as a star that He came, nor as a lightning bolt, nor as a white whale or a holy book or a spirit only, but as a man. And not as many men, not as a series of prophets or divine manifestations, but as one individual: the Messiah, the Holy One of God. Could the Lord ever be said to have been truly human if He had not restricted Himself to one single lifetime, just as He has restricted the rest of us? Yet in that one unique life, in Jesus the centerpiece of the human race, the wild tangent of all the frayed and decrepit flesh of this fallen old world touches perfectly the circle of eternity and is gathered with amazing mercy into it.

NAKEDNESS

The human body, then, possesses a glory that is unique in all the earth (glory in the ordinary sense of "awe-inspiring beauty," but also in the special biblical sense of "the spiritual made visible"), and it is in the peculiar dazzle of nakedness that this glory is most obvious, most tantalizing and revealing. In human nakedness something is uncovered and shown to our eyes and souls that cannot be seen anywhere else, nor even begin to be imitated. The curtain of the holy of holies is pulled aside, and something crouches there in the half-light, something utterly familiar yet stranger than a dream. Human beings are, after all, the only creatures that *can* be naked, the only creatures in which this bizarre unveiling can take place. For in everything else, whether animate or inanimate, nakedness is axiomatic. Trees may be clothed in their autumn splendor or the sea wear a mantle of light—but only by analogy with human clothing. Mankind alone puts an artificial covering over his body. Everything else stands stark, staring naked in the sight of God and is not ashamed.

What is it that sets human nakedness apart from all other nakedness, as something that needs to be covered up? What is so stark about it, so raw and provocative, so intolerable yet at the same time so maddeningly titillating? Why all the embarrassment and secrecy? How did anything ever come to be secret about that most obvious fact of our common existence, this bare flesh of ours with its simple and homely plumbing fixtures? It is as if trees had been declared top secret, or rocks, or as if rivers had private parts, or we dared not look at the sky or the grass for shame. What is this thing called shame, that only humans know? How is it that Nature can be defined as all that exists without it?

There is no very satisfactory explanation for this mystery of shame, except to say that it is inextricably bound up with those other riddles called *evil* and *sin*. The book of Genesis, in fact, traces the history of both clothing and human wickedness back to a common origin: The discovery of sin and the discovery of nakedness appear to have been one and the same event. Before the Fall, "The man and his wife were both naked, and they felt no shame." But once having tasted the forbidden fruit, "The eyes of both of them were opened, and they realized they were naked; so they sewed fig leaves together and made coverings for themselves" (Genesis 2:25; 3:7). The implication is clear: It is not primarily because we get cold or wet that we must cover ourselves up. It was not forty below with blowing snow in Paradise! No, we dress because we sin, and even the finest clothing is like the striped suit of the jailbird, a sign and a reminder that man is an unholy fugitive, in hiding from God and from his own fellows. Whether it be in a nudist colony, at an orgy, in primitive society, or in the nursery, public nudity is possible only for those unconscious or aggressively heedless of their sinfulness. Only the godless and the immature go naked.

The one exception to this rule, of course, is in marriage. Only within this peculiar two-person sanctuary may some of the normal rules and taboos regarding adult nudity be disregarded or relaxed in perfect freedom of conscience. Naturally people have sought loopholes and have discovered many interesting and lurid ways to bend, flout, defy, or exploit moral law. But so powerful a force is nakedness that it is not easily tamed. It tends to dictate its own conditions and stipulations. For to be naked with another person is a sort of picture or symbolic demonstration of perfect honesty, perfect trust, perfect giving and commitment, and if the heart is not naked along with the body, then the whole action becomes a lie and a mockery. It becomes an involvement in an absurd and tragic contradiction: the giving of the body but the withholding of the self. Exposure of the body in a personal encounter is like the telling of one's deepest secret: Afterwards there is no going back, no pretending that the secret is still one's own or that the other does not know. It is, in effect, the ultimate step in human relations, and therefore never one to be taken lightly. It is not a step that establishes deep intimacy but one that presupposes it. As a gesture symbolic of perfect trust and surrender, it requires a setting or structure of perfect surrender in which to take place. It requires the security of the most perfect of reassurances and commitments into which two people can enter, which is no other than the loving contract of marriage.

Even within marriage, of course, there are still restrictions and taboos surrounding nakedness, still uneasiness, shyness, and shame. For sin is everywhere, "crouching at the door" (Genesis 4:7), and it is the special work of sin to destroy trust and intimacy, to bring about enmity and alienation between people. Sin thrives on secrecy, and so it begins by setting up all men and all women in the private little kingdoms of their own hidden bodies, protected from the world behind fortifications of clothing. Even the closest of married couples, like Adam and Eve, are compelled to take refuge in this privacy, hiding not just from the Lord but from one another. The light of nakedness is too intense, it seems, to bask in for very long. Still, though banished from Eden, the first couple were not banished from one another's arms, nor from the marriage bed. This is one garden to which God continues to welcome husbands and wives, and where they are privileged to return again and again in order to expose their nakedness and be healed of secrecy and separateness.

The marriage bed is, in a way, the fleshly counterpart of the confessional, and here it is that bonds of love and trust may be forged that will be strong enough to contend with the sin of shame, which arguably is the deepest and most fundamental sin of all. Why did Adam run from God? "Because I was naked, I was afraid and hid myself," he says (Genesis 3:10). Usually pride, spiritual pride, is given first place as the deadliest of sins. But what is bodily shame but the obverse or underbelly of pride, the flip side of pride's coin? Shame is what a proud man feels when he has nothing left to be proud of. It means continuing to hang on to pride even when every possible basis for pride has disappeared.

And so as pride deceives the soul by ludicrously exalting it, shame deceives the body, the sensual man, by endless accusation and ridicule. Shame takes the loftiest work of God's hands and tries to hide it, or else turns it into something dirty, humiliating, laughable, or embarrassing. Shame makes a double fool of man— first by turning him against his own body and feelings and then by letting him pretend that he can hide. And so he hides behind his fancy clothing (as he does behind his smile), but nothing is really hidden; everyone knows perfectly well what lies underneath. People who see themselves as physically unattractive at least have the advantage of bearing some visible, fleshly reminder of the fallen state of their souls. But in the case of the beautiful, their shame may be buried not just under fine clothing and a smile but beneath the skin itself, and they are the more deceived. Whether we adore our bodies or loathe them, it is still shame that is the master. For shame, essentially, is the guilt and condemnation the soul naturally experiences for having robbed its God, for claiming as its own what is rightfully His. For the body, beautiful or ugly, is the Lord's. It is for Him to bear the shame of it, and for Him to have the glory.

One of the most fundamental and important tasks that has been entrusted to marriage is the work of reclaiming the body for the Lord, of making pure and clean and holy again what has been trampled in the mud of shame. Many artists, it is true, have engaged in the work of recovering some of the sanctity and nobility of the naked body. But what they have attempted to do with paint, husbands and wives do with their own bodies in an unparalleled living canvas of personal risk and commitment. When it comes to the beauty of flesh, husbands and wives are the true artists, the true imagers and interpreters of the body, for they more than anyone else are in a position, earned through love and sacrifice, to see the body as it really is. Under no other circumstances may the vast delight and mystery of nakedness be fully enjoyed and shared in perfect innocence by mature men and women. Were marriage nothing else but this, the role it fulfills among us would still be priceless and irreplaceable. Imagine what anguish it must cause Satan to have to stand aside and watch as married couples discover real pleasure and closeness and love on territory that normally belongs to him!

In our day especially, this unique task of recovering the glory of nakedness, of winning back some of the innocent dignity and solid grandeur of the body as it was originally created out of the dust by our Lord God, is the work of making a silk purse out of a sow's ear, a temple out of a barn. It is the work of giving our naked bodies back to the Creator, through the only practical means available to us, which is the revealing and presenting of ourselves to another person in love. The only way to demonstrate literally that something is not ours is to give it away, and the only way that gesture of giving may be truly generous and sanctified is if it is done in love and in such a way as not to be revoked. In other words, it must be done in accordance with divine ordinance. The free and loving exchange of nakedness that takes place between a husband and wife is just one of the spectacular ways the divine ordinance of holy matrimony actually sets about to reverse the curses of original sin. Marriage attacks original sin, in effect, at its visible root, in the shame of nakedness, and defeats and heals this shame by directly confronting it on the safe and holy ground of a covenant relationship. For a husband and wife to be naked together is like a kind of radiation treatment, the healing rays of which can be felt at the center of the soul. It is, as nearly as possible, a return to the very last statement the book of Genesis makes about mankind's state of innocence in Paradise: "The man and his wife were both naked, and they felt no shame" (Genesis 2:25).

TOUCHING THE CREATOR

What moment in a man's life can compare with that of the wedding night, when a beautiful woman takes off all her clothes and lies next to him in bed, and that woman is his wife? What can equal the surprise of discovering that the one thing above all others that mankind has been most enterprising in dragging through the dirt turns out in fact to be the most innocent thing in the world? Is there any other activity at all in which an adult man and woman may engage together (apart from worship) that is actually more childlike, more clean and pure, more natural and wholesome and unequivocally right than is the act of making love? For if worship is the deepest available form of communion with God (and especially that particular act of worship known as Communion), then surely sex is the deepest communion possible between human beings, and as such is something absolutely essential (in more than a biological or procreative way) to the survival of the race.

So far we have spoken of sex only in relation to nakedness, as if it were a thing of seeing rather than of touching. And yet where else is our faculty of touch more lavishly concentrated than in the act of sex? Touch is what it's all about—and not only external touching, skin against skin, but touching of the insides as well, of organs and juices. Nevertheless, as dependent as sex is upon touch, it is still something that begins, like lust, in the eyes. The first move is a movement of the eyes, and the first contact is eye contact. "The eye is the lamp of the body," taught Jesus. "If your eyes are good, your whole body will be full of light" (Matthew 6:22). He was not talking about physical eyes, of course, but about the faculty of "seeing," which is our power of understanding. If we have a right understanding, right actions will follow. In the case of sex, we need to begin with a right understanding of our bodies. We need to see in nakedness what God intended us to see: the glory of His presence in the world, the highest expression of what He Himself looks like, the very form that He assumed when He visited the earth in person. Can we not detect His own paint still wet on our skins, and the marks of His fingers imprinted in our ears, in our eye sockets, on our lips, and on our genitals? Only when we perceive that these poor bodies of ours are the natural (as opposed to supernatural) expression of God's glory, so that nakedness is as close as most of us will ever get to seeing God in the flesh, only then can we begin to understand also that sex is the closest thing (next to the Eucharist) to touching Him.

The story is told of a young pastor who went to visit an old hermit renowned for his saintliness. Late at night, the elder man suggested they go for a walk on the hillside. Out in the open, under the stars, with darkness close all around them, suddenly the hermit said, "Let us kneel and pray," and they did. Telling of it later, the young man recalled, "I was afraid to stretch out my hand in the darkness in case I should touch God."

That is something of what it is like for a man to be near a woman, or a woman near a man: It is to know the holy fear of reaching out and doing the very thing one longs most to do. It is to be afraid, not merely from social taboo, but out of the sudden realization that this thing is too holy, that one is not good enough for it and never can be. It is to expect rejection and yet to be received. But who is good enough to receive another person's body as a gift? And who is not afraid at the thought of having to make an adequate return for such a gift? Sex is not like holding hands (it is nothing so sane as that): It is more like cutting the hands off, with perfect abandon, and throwing them into the sea. It is like being on a dark hillside, and suddenly closer than one ever dreamed of getting to something that is so big and pure that one cannot even begin to take it in. And then the whole hillside moves—not away, but closer still. It is to experience a feeling that behaves in many ways like fear, except that it is indescribably delicious. Of all the sensations we can experience with our physical senses, surely this is the one that comes closest to the Lord's Supper in being an actual touching of the source of our being, of our Creator.

For many people, certainly, sex is the most powerful and moving experience that life has to offer, and more overwhelmingly holy than anything that happens in church. For great masses of people, sex is the one force that can actually tip men and women completely off their accustomed centers of gravity and lift them, however briefly, right out of themselves. And it is one place in life in which the lion really does seem to lie down with the lamb: the lion of our corrupt, violent, and sinful flesh with the lamb of love and innocence. As the poet Yeats expressed this paradox, "Love has pitched his mansion in the place of excrement." Sex is one of those things that may force a man to his knees (or at least onto his back or stomach), and precisely because the act is so undignified, so ridiculous, so degrading, and so implicitly dirty, it possesses also the capacity to be cleansing and transcendent.

Anything that rubs people's noses in their mortality is also capable of lifting their hearts to God, and probably no other phenomena on earth are so effective in this respect as are that great trio of death, prayer, and sex. Like prayer, sex is a thing of exertion, of sweat, and of groaning, and like death, it is intimately acquainted with surrender, with excretion, and with the mournful frailty and heartrending glory of flesh. And these are all things that God has made. He made the woman with an open wound in her body, such that it can be stanched only by a man; and the man He made with a tumor, the maddening pressure of which is alleviated only when it is allowed to grow inside the woman's wound. He made the man to root and to flower in the aching earth of a woman. He made sex, we have cause to suspect, specifically so that it would be difficult for the mind of man to conceive of anything more earthy, more humiliating, or more desirable, and so to be a constant reminder to him of his true nature. But it was also to instruct him in a higher nature and in his destiny. For in touching a person of the opposite sex in the most secret place of his or her body, with one's own most private part, there is something that reaches beyond touch, that gets behind flesh itself to the place where it connects with spirit, to the place where incarnation happens.

"The Holy Spirit will come upon you," the angel told Mary, "and the power of the Most High will overshadow you" (Luke 1:35). Jesus Christ was born to a virgin, not in order to sidestep the messy and embarrassing business of intercourse, but in order that the Lord Himself might be directly involved in it. Sex is a scandal that the Most High has chosen to consecrate through His own participation.

Angel and Animal

Surely it was God's full intention for the physical joining together of a man and a woman to be one of the mountaintop experiences of life, one of those summit points of both physical and mystical rapture in which He Himself might overshadow His people in love, might come down among them and be most intimately and powerfully revealed. How horribly tragic, therefore, that it is at this very point, here at this precious male-female encounter that ought to be overflowing with holiness, here that godless people have succeeded in descending to some of the most abysmal levels of human degradation. Yet what a high price is paid for the least cheapening of a gift so full of beauty and grace and power! Sex inescapably is one of the holiest shrines of life, a crossroads of towering spiritual intensity where simple but monumental decisions are made and acted out, choices that have earth-shattering ramifications for every detail of a life. The most casual of sexual liaisons may be like some great submarine earthquake, sending its slow and unfathomable shock waves not only into every corner of the lives of the lovers themselves but throughout the entire nexus of family and friends, extending even to the unborn and to whole future generations. Sex is sacred ground. It is a place where men may turn themselves into animals as effortlessly as a magician waves a wand, or else may begin to be transformed into the children of God. It is, more conspicuously than anywhere else, the place where the angel and the animal in man meet face to face, and engage in mortal struggle. One of them must die.

Marriage is the only weapon man possesses against the brutalizing passion, the pitiless and primitive energy, the mindless biological explosiveness of the raw sex drive. Marriage in itself, of course, is not a charm that automatically works either to civilize, to sanctify, or even to medicate intercourse. Perhaps it is only slightly more difficult for sex to be animalized within marriage than outside of it. But the word *slightly* is important: For even if every marriage bed on earth were to be defiled, the very existence of marriage as a mere concept, as a relic of the dim past, as an unattainable ideal of faithfulness and purity in sexual relations, would continue to heap burning coals upon the head of profligacy. As it is, any marriage in which sex is abused and twisted can hardly be expected to last for long or to provide any real fulfillment, but on the contrary can bring only condemnation. Sex is a powerful outward symbol of the inner temper of a marital relationship. It is an arresting and self-evident truth that the quality of a marriage in all of its facets depends upon a wholesome and mutually satisfying sex life. And the corollary is also true, that the partners' feelings about the marriage as a whole will almost always be reflected in the quality of their sexual relations.

For some people it may be difficult or disturbing to have to admit that the fleshly body plays such a predominant, and even a preeminent, role in spiritual life. But for the godly and the ungodly alike, it is nevertheless the case that physical existence is the sphere in which spiritual truth must be worked out. While sex is not the only aspect of physical relationship in a marriage, it is in most cases the most important one, the touchstone for everything else from smiles and daily gestures of tenderness to deeds of kindness and sacrifice. In sheer power and passion, the physical love life tends to be way out ahead of all other expressions of love between a couple. The rest of marriage lags behind, and in many ways the whole challenge of marital life is simply to catch up in all other departments with the pure rapture of the physical relationship at its best.

If couples could give themselves to one another in every way as they did when they first passionately embraced, or as they have in their most sublime experiences of sex, or even in their most ordinary lovemaking, then their problems would be few. What great and profound truths, what startling confessions and intimacies pass between the hearts of a man and a woman when they are in bed together! It may have taken hours of sensitive closeness and patience, of tentative explorations, and literally hundreds of kisses and hugs and strokings and subtle contacts and pressures between the two bodies of wife and husband before they were able to enter into a place of such extraordinary honesty and simplicity and naked safety, into that still point of absolute trust at the heart of the sanctuary of sex. But perhaps the ultimate test of their love will lie in whether or not they can believe in those times of almost perfect giving and acceptance, believe in them as being the true times, the holy times, never doubting or resenting or forgetting them afterwards in the stress and trial of daily life, but rather building on them, taking them as the models of what their love must be (and really is in its essence), nurturing and enlarging those deep seeds of intimacy that have been so lovingly planted in the memory of their flesh.

At the same time it should be clear that sex must never be depended upon to establish love but can only grow out of it. And while problems in a sexual relationship may sometimes be overcome simply through a deeper knowledge of basic physiology or through the introduction of new techniques, such improvements will be short lived if they are not backed up by profound changes in attitude at the emotional and spiritual level. For sex is one of those mysteries that, like prayer, will not yield to technique, and any approach with a view to technical mastery will be doomed from the start. What the sex life really demands is the loving gift of the self, the sincere devotion of the whole heart. Where this is present, problems such as impotence, premature ejaculation, or inability to achieve orgasm will fade into insignificance and in time may well disappear. Only love can really cope with (let alone heal) such things, but without love the greatest prowess and technical success in lovemaking will procure about as much true satisfaction as there is in a mouthful of sawdust.

In short, where there are sexual problems in a marriage, the answer is not usually to be found in the pages of a handbook or in the office of a sex therapist (although such counsel has its place), but rather in patience and purity of love, and in a sincere turning toward God. If a couple were to seek the Lord with their whole will, rejoice in Christian fellowship, and spend time both alone and together in heartfelt prayer and study of the Scriptures, they would soon find their love life filled with a rich glow and a mysterious new energy that cannot be discovered through any worldly means. For as the Lord is the author of sex, so He is its interpreter, and His therapy is most to be treasured.

VIVE LA DIFFERENCE!

In the final analysis, the force or phenomenon we have been calling by the name of sex turns out to be fundamentally the same phenomenon as that of marriage itself: It is the phenomenon of magnetism, of two opposite poles attracting. One of the greatest challenges facing a marriage is for the partners to accept this inherent oppositeness between them and to allow the poles to exist and in a certain sense to *remain apart,* rather than always striving to force them together. Inevitably, as we shall see, a couple will grow more and more like one another in character. Yet at the same time, for two to become one flesh does not mean for the hand to become a foot. It means, rather, for the foot and the hand to become coordinated, to start doing the same task, heading in the same direction.

It is a dangerous thing in marriage to forget, even for a moment, that one's partner is a person of the opposite sex. This may sound like a preposterous unlikelihood, but in fact it is precisely what tends to happen in a marriage; just as cohabitation can at times serve to heighten the psychological differences between people, so also can it serve to flatten the anatomical ones. That very depth of intimacy that is the soul of a relationship can become its most insidious enemy, as a couple may be lulled into assuming that they are far more similar, in every way, than they really are. Continual togetherness, predictability of behavior, and just the routine sameness of everyday life are all factors that constantly threaten to blur the compelling distinction between man and woman that is the salt of marriage and the reason for the whole drama of attraction in the first place. The result is that couples can end up arguing over some of the very differences that initially fascinated them, or else assuming there is agreement in areas where agreement is not even desirable.

So it can be important for a husband to remember that his wife is a creature vastly different from himself, not simply a different person, but a *woman:* almost, indeed, an alien being! Of course the woman is not an alien being at all, but a human being. Still, she is a different *kind* of human from the man, and that means she is bound to have a different way of looking at things, different categories of thoughts, different shades of emotion, some different needs, and so on. Naturally many things about her will be strange just because she is a different person from her husband; but the strangeness will be augmented, or lifted onto another plane, by the simple fact that she is a woman and not a man. When people forget that the opposite sex is opposite, it can result in men actually resenting women for not being men, and vice versa. Ultimately this is just one aspect of the way in which people are continually being hoodwinked into assuming they are in relationship with one another, when really all they are relating to is themselves. And there is neurosis in a nutshell.

Let it be remembered, then, that a magnet has two poles, and if it does not, then it has lost its magnetism. This sad situation can come about in many ways in a marriage, but one of the greatest danger signals is when either partner no longer feels physically attracted to the other. Then the magnet has lost its pull, and it is nothing but a useless hunk of scrap iron. This essential attraction has nothing to do, as is commonly supposed, with youth or sex appeal or normal standards of beauty. It is a matter purely of male and female and of the image of God. When a Christian man can no longer feel attracted to his wife, the chances are that he will also soon lose interest in his God. What has happened is that he actually forgets (as incredible as this may sound) that his wife is a woman. And once a man fails to appreciate his wife as a woman, the next step is that he forgets she is a full-fledged person. And then he forgets that he himself is a man. And then he has lost everything.

The institution of matrimony is founded not just upon the principle that men and women are dependent one upon the other, but that at a level much more profound and mysterious, maleness and femaleness are themselves interdependent. There can be no maleness without femaleness, and femaleness without maleness would likewise be at a total loss as to how to define itself. Marriage, therefore, and specifically that bizarre and beautiful marriage of naked bodies in intercourse, is in a very succinct and real way a definition of humanity: "Male and female He created them" (Genesis 1:27).

THE CLOTH-COVERED DANCING HORSE

Besides being a way of defining humanity, sexual intercourse is also, strangely enough, a way of defining God. For to call God the Author of sex, as we have, is not just to say that He invented it, as He invented or created everything else in the world. It is to say, more importantly, that sexual love has its source in God's own being, in His nature, and that in the same way that human beings, body and soul, are a unique reflection in this world of God's very self and character, so the sex act itself may be said to be in God's likeness, fashioned in His own image.

In the beginning, after all, the two genders were already joined in one physical body, and in order to separate them into two individuals the Lord had to perform a surgical operation: "He caused the man to fall into a deep sleep; and while he was sleeping, He took part of the man's side...and made a woman" (Genesis 2:21–22). The woman was not made from the dust or out of nothing, but rather was taken out of the man and in such a way that physically the man became a somewhat different and perhaps even a lesser creature. If nothing else, he lost a rib. But we sense that the change may have been a more radical and extensive one than that.

In any case it is the male and the female together who constitute the image of God, in a more profound sense than either of them standing alone, and sexual intercourse remains as an emblem and an actual remnant of the original condition of humanity as it first emerged from the dust, fresh-formed in the Lord's hand. And while an unmarried individual may travel quite readily toward eternal life encased in a single physical body, the married couple contracts to undertake this same voyage in the joint body of matrimony. They take each step together or not at all. They are *one flesh,* and they need to learn to think and to walk that way. Little wonder that the world of a new marriage is every bit as strange as the world of a newborn baby! The couple too has a brand-new body to get used to—and a two-headed, four-footed body at that!

There is something amphibious about marriage, something neither fish nor fowl. It is like a three-legged sack race or a cloth-covered dancing horse, except that it is not only the feet and body but one's whole being that gets tangled up in the other person's. Marriage is not just a sharing but a mingling of identities, a consanguinity of psyches. It is a blend so intimate that it actually becomes hard to tell where one person leaves off and the other begins. People will peer and peer, for example, at a couple's offspring, trying to determine which one of the parents they resemble. Perhaps in a mysterious way what they are really trying to do is to tell the couple themselves apart, to separate again what has become impossibly intertwined.

Not that this uncanny congruity of the flesh of inner lives is always a very obvious or noticeable fact; but it becomes conspicuous in the birth of a child or at other times of crisis or exposure, those times when the hidden realities of lives float suddenly and dramatically to the surface. It becomes plain as day, for example, when either of the partners dies. Then it is perfectly apparent how much of one's own precious lifeblood has been gambled away upon the heart of another, and how much, for the moment, one appears to have lost the wager. At any point in the journey of matrimony, the Lord may decide to take away from us the very one we have given ourselves up to, and such a loss is felt at first not as the loss of another person but rather as the loss of a part of ourselves. A bereaved spouse is like a person struck blind, or one who has lost limbs or been left without any feeling in the nerves. It is for the Lord, and for Him only, to heal such a wound, to "close up the place with flesh."

WALTZ OF CELLS

Neither in death, however, nor in the birth of a child, nor anywhere else is the inextricable interconnectedness of the married couple made more plain, more visible and tangible, than in the act of sex. Here the incredible dancing horse, the beast with two backs, the two-gendered, one-fleshed human creature of Genesis, becomes a literal reality. The Bible does not promise that marriage in itself will bring about one mind or one heart in a couple, but it does teach most emphatically that the marriage of bodies in sexual intercourse results in a man and a woman becoming one flesh. Writes Paul, "Do you not know that he who unites himself with a prostitute is one with her in body?" (1 Corinthians 6:16). So apparently it is not the marriage vows alone, but more specifically the act of intercourse that brings about this extraordinary union.

For the genitals, positioned as they are, can hardly be engaged without the rest of the body following suit, and even as toes and fingers interlace, so noses, eyelids, lips, and tongues splay and press against one another in an act that is visibly, as well as emotionally and spiritually, a passionate effort to unite. Even the simple act of kissing is powerfully symbolic of the crush of personalities, as each partner pushes his features against those of the other as if to make one new face out of the two. Kissing implies losing face; it is inherently a free and wholehearted gesture of self-effacement.

Much more than being a symbolic gesture, however, much more than a sign, intercourse is a seal. In an obvious way it is a literal union of sweat and spittle, excretion and secretion, flecks and rubbings of all sorts of tissues. Less obviously, it is a union of cells, of genes and hormones, of neurons and corpuscles and electrons, and of less substantial bits as well: particles of personality, molecules of memory, brain bits and soul scrapings, to say nothing of whole clouds of emotion. Copulation is an activity that (uniquely in humans) comes close to being a systematic touching and stroking of every square millimeter of two bodies, and one that a man and a woman almost literally have to turn themselves inside out in order to perform. If this is not quite what actually takes place, it is at least what the lovers appear to be striving for, as each seems intent upon stripping off their very skin and wrapping it around the other. Sex is a cheek-to-cheek waltz of cells across the hormone-polished dance floor of flesh. It is almost as if every atom of one body were to be lined up against every atom in the other body in a one-to-one correspondence, and then vigorously rubbed together. And how the sparks do fly!

It is little wonder, with so much going on at the purely biological level, that what is meanwhile being whispered in the ear of the soul is no sweet nothing; on the contrary, it is almost everything there is, as much of one whole person as can possibly be squeezed into another. What happens visibly and corporeally in sex cannot help but resonate in the deepest chambers of temperament, psyche, and spirit. Inevitably what this means is that there is a total nakedness between two people: nakedness not just of flesh, of touch, of eyes, but of feelings, of ideas, and of all the faintest stirrings of the soul.

We may not think of the removal of clothes as being a revelation of our thoughts and character, but that, in fact, is exactly what happens. Just as the self-consciousness of nakedness, which is the shame of sin, renders it more difficult for man to hide himself from God, so the frank exposure of that nakedness in sex makes it much harder for a man and a woman to hide anything at all from one another. They may *think* they can still hide and keep secrets, but in truth they cannot, for they have become one flesh as surely as if their very nervous systems had been coupled together into the same computer network. Thereafter, what one knows, the other knows also with the deep and secret knowledge of the flesh, and they needn't kid themselves that this is not the case. Whenever anything is wrong, they will both know it and will both react. When it comes to any secret, a husband may well be able to conceal from his wife *what* it is, exactly, but he can never hide the fact *that* it is. For the effects of it will already be flashing automatically through all the electronic circuits of her bone marrow. It is probable that not the slightest hint of a shadow passes across a husband's eyes that does not darken also the eyes of his wife.

For this is what is always and inevitably involved in the making of love.

SIX

rather be right than happy?

Submission

Submit to one another

out of reverence for Christ.

—EPHESIANS 5:21

Submission

CASTLE OR MONASTERY?

"The LORD gives, and the LORD takes away; blessed be the Name of the LORD" (Job 1:21).

Marriage, like life itself, is both a giving and a taking away. What is given in marriage is fairly obvious: the love of another human being. What is taken away is perhaps not quite so apparent: the entire freedom to think and to act as an independent person. If people understood exactly how radical is the curtailment of independence in marriage, there could never be any thought of divorce. Divorce would be seen as a form of suicide. But then, if people understood the true depth of self-abnegation that marriage demands, there would perhaps be far fewer weddings. For marriage, too, would be seen as a form of suicide. It would be seen not as a way of augmenting one's comfort and security in life, but rather as a way of losing one's life for the sake of Christ.

One of the commonest illusions about marriage is that it is meant to be a sanctuary, a place of familiarity and protectedness amidst the alien harshness of the world, a place in which the rigors of change and challenge and uncertainty are expected to be minimized, the shocks of life abated. Home is a place to put one's feet up, to rest, to be free from struggle, and to a large extent all of this is true. God wants us to enjoy security. Unfortunately, we have a way of equating security with complacency. "A man's home is his castle," goes the saying, and in practice this is taken to mean that a man is allowed and even encouraged to develop into any sort of despot or devil he likes within the cozy confines, the cordoned lawlessness, of his own family. After all, aren't his loved ones those who understand and accept him? And so marriage becomes a form of institutionalized complacency, a hothouse of mutually nourished neuroses. Love is even construed to be a sort of carte blanche approval for all kinds of selfishness and evil, a dispensation giving two people special license to sin against one another.

Yet holy matrimony, like other holy orders, was never intended as a comfort station for lazy people. On the contrary, it is a systematic program of deliberate and thoroughgoing self-sacrifice. A man's home is not his castle so much as his monastery, and if he happens to be treated like a king there, then it is only so that he might better be enabled to become a servant. For marriage is intended to be an environment in which he will be lovingly yet persistently confronted with the plainest and ugliest evidence of his sinfulness, and thus encouraged on a daily basis to repent and to change. Marriage is really a drastic course of action that, as much as any monastic commitment, dedicates the votary to a life of vigorous self-denial, to a disciplined path of renunciation and of retreat from the world. It is a radical step and is not intended for anyone who is not prepared, indeed eager, to surrender his own will and to be wholeheartedly submissive to the will of another. For there is no way to surrender the will except by surrendering it to another will. And there is no way to attack the root of selfishness except by disciplining and subduing that determined monster of self-aggrandizement known as the human will.

In marriage it so happens that the Lord has devised a particularly gentle (but no less disciplined and effective) means for helping men and women to humble themselves, to surrender their errant wills. Even the closest of couples will inevitably find themselves engaged in a struggle of wills, for marriage is a wild, audacious attempt at an almost impossible degree of cooperation between two powerful centers of self-assertion. Marriage cannot help being a furnace of conflict, a crucible in which these two wills must be melted down and purified and made to conform. Most people do not realize that this is what they are signing up for when they get married, but this is what invariably faces them.

Marriage turns out to be through and through an act of acquiescence, a willing compliance, both with God and with one other person, in the difficult process of one's own subdual and mortification. It cannot succeed without, first of all, a profound acceptance of the conditions of struggle, the state of personal siege, in which it must be lived out, and secondly, without an ever-growing realization that one's own self cannot and must not emerge as the winner of this struggle. "He who is least among you," says Jesus, "he is the greatest" (Luke 9:48), and marriage at its best is a sort of contest in what might be called "one-downmanship," a backwards tug of war between two wills each equally determined not to win. That is really the only attitude that works in marriage because that is the way the Lord designed it. He planned it especially as a way for men and women to enter wholeheartedly, with full consent and consequent peace and joy, into the inevitable process of their own diminishment, which is His worship and glorification. For "He must increase, but I must decrease," declared John the Baptist of Jesus (John 3:30), and that is the fate of all of us: We must all diminish for the glory of God.

PLANNED OBSOLESCENCE

From one point of view, the whole of life may be seen as a taking away, as one long and painful series of subtractions. We are forever being called upon to pull up stakes, to release our hold upon the things and places and people we have loved and even upon each precious second as it slips through our aging fingers. Our very bodies are like tents, says Paul (2 Corinthians 5:1), the most temporary of houses, and our whole existence under the sun bears the marks of exile and nomadism. If we are lucky enough to survive into old age, it will only be to find that even the most basic amenities of life will begin to be withdrawn from us one by one: legal freedoms; good health; friends; the comforts of our own home; physical and intellectual abilities; the capacity to think clearly, remember things, read a book, walk around the block, enjoy food, go to the bathroom. An old man is a ruined city, a fallen kingdom, a disaster area full of leaks and potholes and crumbling walls. In the end there may be nothing left to him but life itself, the faintest squiggle on a piece of graph paper, and even that may be unceremoniously flicked away like a speck of lint from the collar of the dashing young world.

There is no escaping this fate, no circumventing our planned obsolescence in this world. There is no discipline that will appease it, no faith that will reverse it, no bargaining nor even love that can buy it off. Tragically, so large and real looms this specter of unrelenting decay that for many people it is the only side of life they ever see. How many go down to death in bitterness, resentment, and rage! For life appears to them to have been utterly impersonal and mechanistic, and therefore meaningless. If any personal or meaningful pattern is discernible at all, then it is a malignant one, designed specifically to attack them, to weaken and humiliate, gradually to kick away all of the props and finally to leave them without anything at all to stand on. By waging so pitiful a struggle not to become obsolete, when in reality the whole natural flow of physical life is toward obsolescence, what people really do is to declare a preference for temporal values over eternal ones. What they do, in fact, is to reject the kingdom of God and its gift of eternal life.

As it turns out, the only way not to reject eternal values is to submit willingly to the erosion of temporal ones. "Take kindly the counsel of the years, gracefully surrendering the things of youth," says Max Ehrmann in his poem, "Desiderata." A spirit of graceful submission is required of every person in life, and there can be no peace without it. For one way or another we must all be humbled, even unto death. One way or another we must all die a little every day, and in the process we will all suffer unspeakably.

A Face to Suffering

Marriage is no shelter against this hard fact. It is not a little bastion of tenderness designed to soften the blows of fate. It is not a clever system of protection in which another person is interposed between ourselves and the pain of living. On the contrary, the person interposed may actually become the source or focus of more suffering than we ever bargained for, the very vessel from which our own humiliation is poured. Is it not a bitter and ironic truth that the very person we love most in the world may appear to us, from time to time, to be the only thing standing between ourselves and our happiness? Not only does marriage fail to mitigate the struggles of life, but there is a way in which it actually deepens them, rendering them even more poignant, because more personal. Just as the man who loves God will almost certainly incur greater suffering in this world than the man who does not, so it is that a man who loves a woman may, by virtue of that very fact, open himself up to deeper levels of suffering than a man who will not commit himself to any love at all. For it is not in the nature of love to deflect pain, but rather to absorb it, and to absorb greater and greater amounts of it. Marriage gives a face to suffering, just as it gives a face to joy, and thereby enables the suffering not to be lessened but rather to be transformed from something inhuman and faceless into something fully human, something that registers in the depths of relational personhood. It is true of all intimacy, but especially of marriage, that it creates the unique and miraculous circumstances in which suffering cannot be extricated from love.

The truth about marriage is that it is a way not of avoiding any of the painful trials and subtractions of life but rather of confronting them, of exposing and tackling them most intimately, most humanly. It is a way to meet suffering personally, head-on, with the peculiar directness, the reckless candidness characteristic only of love. It is a way of living life with no other strategy or defense or protection than that of love. And so it is the gradual unfolding of an amazing process of interpersonal consecration, a process in which all the pain locked up in two lonely, self-centered lives is no longer hidden or suppressed (as it tends to be everywhere else in life) but rather released, released so that in the hands of love it might be used as the raw material for sanctification. Marriage is a way not to evade suffering, but to suffer purposefully.

That is why matrimony may correctly be termed a holy order, a special category, in fact, of the religious life. It is a monasticism in which the vow and discipline of chastity becomes the vow and discipline of fidelity, in which the vow of poverty is translated into an unqualified sharing of the totality of one's life and possessions, in which the vow of stability applies not to a place or a fraternity but to a particular person, and in which the vow of obedience is practiced not in community but in partnership and not toward a superior but to an equal. In matrimony, as in other holy orders, the meaning of *holy* is interpreted in the light of its homonym *wholly:* For only through wholeness of dedication can human life begin to approach holiness.

Forsaking All Others

How does this work in practice? How is marriage, apparently so worldly an option when set beside celibacy, actually a path not only of wholehearted dedication but of self-denial and retreat from the world?

Right from the start, it should be clear that the very act of selecting a lifetime mate and settling down is a sort of throwing in of the towel, a deliberate choice to be put on the shelf, out of circulation. Not everyone realizes this at the time they enter into marriage, but sooner or later it does become apparent (in one of a thousand surprising ways) that in choosing to be married one has also chosen not to be single, and that in choosing one particular partner one has automatically surrendered the possibility of marrying anyone else. The field, in short, has with one fell swoop been alarmingly narrowed, and it is probably true in general that the decision to be married has the effect of closing more doors than any other single decision in life. Other doors may be opened, it is true, but in a very real sense the whole future course of a married person's life is delimited and informed by the character, aspirations, and destiny of one other human being, one out of all the other billions on the earth.

Furthermore, it should be clear that anyone who enters into marriage actually relinquishes the right to engage in any other adult relationship that might be equally deep or pervasive. One chooses one's mate as one chooses one's God: forsaking all others, until death. It is a true renunciation of all the rest of the world, "keeping me only unto thee."

But this is only the beginning of the renunciation in which marriage involves us. This is only the first step. Thereafter, the whole of married life may be seen as a working out of the implications and consequences of this initial and drastic step of renunciation, which is not so much the taking of another person to ourselves as it is the giving of ourselves to the other, the giving up of ourselves for the other's sake. For in marriage we do not give ourselves to a cause or a program or a belief, but to a person, assuming all the complex and incalculable risks that surrender entails. From now on, the greatest part of all the "giving in" and "letting go" we must do in life will be done within the context of our marriage, as we surrender not only to the Lord but to our human partner, and as we are called on to let go not only of all the worldliness we ourselves cling to but of everything that clings to the other as well, every fleshly desire, every weakness, every sin. If it is hard to accept our own imperfection, then it is harder still to accept imperfection in another. And if there is anything more painful than having to acquiesce in the inevitable process of our own decline, our deterioration into death, then it is watching the same process at work in the one we love.

Is a wife going bald, losing her curves, her good looks? Then her husband must renounce his attachment to those things, at just as deep a level as the wife herself must do. Rather than lamenting the loss of her youth, both must learn to rejoice in the new and more lasting thing that comes into being precisely because of the attitude of graceful submission the couple must develop in the face of the advancing years. For this new thing is the deeper love they discover, a love not dependent upon any earthly thing at all.

Or let us say that the husband develops a serious illness and is bedridden for the rest of his life: Will the wife be able to accept this external change in his manliness, yet still treat him as a man? Will she be able to acquiesce in her new role as nurse, caring lovingly for his needs, and yet refraining from mothering him? Will she be able to tolerate the frustration and anger that will almost certainly grip her husband in his sickness? And will the man be able to accept his wife's care?

These are all questions of submission. No marriage can succeed unless it is permeated, saturated, with this spirit of acquiescence, of continual giving in, of gracious and willing compliance. As we have seen, such a spirit demands to be cultivated by every person, whether single or married, in every area of life. But marriage adds a unique dimension to this struggle, in that the submission we are called upon to exercise is not only to sickness or to old age or death, nor to parents or government or society at large, nor to any system or institution, nor to natural law or to any law at all, nor even (directly) to God, but rather to another human being, and particularly to one we ourselves have selected and promised to love. It is submission not to anything external or imposed, but only to what we ourselves have chosen with our whole hearts. It is submission not merely to the vicissitudes of life, but to those particular vicissitudes, those disillusionments, those injustices, those bitter insecurities, those upsets, and all those felt cruelties of the world as they happen to be expressed in and through the being of another person. Everything about marriage is personalized—the joy, but also the pain. Marriage is not the sharp corner of a table banging into your side but a person speaking a sharp word to you. It is not waving your fist into an empty sky but rather into a human face, into the face of your own love. It is not the graying of

hair or the stiffening of muscles; it is the person you love looking
at you as if suddenly you are old or ugly or a piece of excess baggage.

PERSONAL AUTHORITY

If this unrelenting personalness, this extremity of intimacy, is the
greatest blessing of marriage, it is also its point of greatest stress.
For there is one underlying principle deeply encrusted in fallen
human nature that probably bears more responsibility than any
other single factor for the difficulties experienced in marriage. That
principle says, quite simply, that people will much more readily
submit themselves to an impersonal authority than to a personal
one. A man seeking good advice, for example, is more likely to follow the advice contained in a book of his own choosing than that
offered face-to-face by a trusted friend. Or again, a man who may
docilely comply with all sorts of humiliating conditions in his
workplace will bitterly resent one unjust word spoken by his boss.
Boss and *workplace* are perceived as two qualitatively different
embodiments of authority. What is important is not so much the
demands that are placed upon people but the source of those
demands, and a personal source is more questionable and offensive
than an impersonal one.

The reason for this phenomenon is not too hard to discern, for
at heart people like to think of themselves as their own boss, and
an impersonal or collective authority allows them to fool themselves into believing that this is actually the case. When the leader
is invisible, a follower may conclude that it is really himself who is
calling the shots, and the resulting cooperation may have more to
do with sleepwalking than with any true and voluntary attitude of
obedience. When the leader is visible, on the other hand, and takes

the form of a fellow human, then the very idea of obedience arouses suspicion. Outside of well-defined structures, there is little place in Western culture for the compliance of one individual with the will of another. That is not the way things work. And so the principle holds true in all areas of life, that we are generally more subservient to corporate than to personal rule, to groups rather than to individuals. We are more willing to obey laws than people.

When it comes to marriage, therefore, we are faced with a problem, for nowhere is the issue of acquiescence to the will of another individual more germane. No compliance is more personal or more necessary than that required in marriage. There is no more intimate expression of authority in our lives, and certainly none of which it is truer that we ourselves have given the authorization for it. Yet for that very reason, there is no other power than that of our own spouse against which we are quicker to rebel. For if we were the ones who authorized it in the beginning, then surely it ought to remain under our control? And yet it is of the essence of love to relinquish control, as Jesus did when He placed Himself in the hands of the Jewish and Roman authorities. Christian love, in fact, acknowledges the only true authority there is—the authority of God the Father—not by resisting all other authorities, but by surrendering to them. The Christian puts himself entirely into the hands of the Lord by putting himself entirely into the hands of worldly authority, for the world "would have no power if it had not been given from above" (John 19:11). So love lets God rule, and ultimately love *gains* control precisely by means of *relinquishing* control, by means of obedience, submission, servanthood.

For anyone able to accept this strategy of Christian love, the extra demands placed upon obedience and renunciation within the context of marriage are no threat but rather a tremendous blessing. For while the demands imposed by the world tend to hide behind cloaks of abstraction, impersonality, and bureaucracy ("Don't blame me, mister; I'm only doing my job"), the claims of marriage are the claims of one particular human heart over another. The special gift of marriage, in fact, is that the submissiveness asked of us is not to anything alien or abstract, but rather to a person; nor is it to a distant and unknown person, but to the one closest to us; nor is our deference to be one of blind following but of love.

Such obedience ought to be the easiest of all, but instead, as we have seen, it can turn out to be the most difficult. The difficulty is not an inherent one, but one manufactured by our own willfulness when it becomes clear, under the steady eye of intimacy, that what is being asked of us is nothing short of the surrender of our very will to (or rather, through) another person. Many a man will surrender his whole life to alcohol or to some ideology or to money or ambition or to the glamour of politics long before he would think of surrendering to his wife. The difficulty in marriage is that there is no chance or illusion that what one is really surrendering to may be oneself. No, one's selfish willfulness has a definite opponent, an enemy with flesh and blood and will of its own, residing under one's own roof, sleeping in the same bed.

THE BLACK AND WHITE OF LOVE

The problem most couples experience is that marriage is not *abstract* enough. Its demands, just like the demands of the Christian faith, are altogether too specific, too moral. For when Christ enters a person's life, it is always on the level of morality, and everyday morality at that. It is not religious transports or ecstasies that He deals in primarily, but rather in placing His finger on this or on that particular mess in our lives—on this insult to a friend, on that little white lie or piece of gossip. And so it is in marriage, that where the pressure is felt most is in a whole series of tiny, sharply defined issues of morality, issues that even have a tendency to take the shape of commandments: do not squeeze the toothpaste from the top; honor the day of your anniversary; remember to take out the garbage; don't use the power saw when your wife is home because she can't stand the noise; and so on. It is a whole bunch of really *little* things that can ruin a marriage, because that is what our wills tend to be made up of: petty, selfish desires. Only another person can challenge and confront us at this deep personal level of our own private will and reveal to us how petty it is. Only a real encounter with another real person, day in and day out, can begin to prick the bubble of the ego.

Demands that are just as concrete and specific as those of marriage can, of course, be made by society at large or by any number of other interests and concerns, but at least in these cases we may take comfort in the notion that whatever sacrifices we are asked to make are for the good of the group as a whole. In marriage, however, we are called on to make sacrifices for the sake of just one person, and our constant question is, why should I? What's the point? Isn't *my* say-so just as important as *hers?* There is none of the pressure of mass culture or group dynamics or mere conformity. We must perform real sacrifices, daily, at the level of personal will. Huge and impossible issues of morality are narrowed to a pinpoint in marriage, defined precisely and concretely so that our response to them must be made precisely and concretely. Love etches in black and white, hones to a fine edge. There is no shadow, no place to hide behind vague abstractions. Marriage reduces all decisions to one, one simple decision that must be made over and over, and there are no results more particular or far-reaching or catastrophic than the results of that initial and ongoing decision to invite one other person to interfere permanently in our lives.

The continual intimate presence and pressure of this one other will in our lives exercises a power that turns out to be far more pervasive than any other of the world's influences. Certainly it is more profound in its effects than any set of corporate or impersonal factors, whether they be those of business, government, or even culture. For the human psyche knows no influence that is more penetrating than that of one single personality upon another, and it is within the bond of marriage that this potential for personal impact comes into fullest bloom. There is simply no other power in the world like the power that a husband and a wife have over one another. If you wish to leave the indelible stamp of your own character and spirit upon another human being, the way to do it best is not through teaching or discipleship, and certainly not through hypnosis or black magic or political power, and not even through parenting, but rather through marriage: that is, through the unique combination of blood with covenant. For marriage is recognized throughout the world, in nearly all cultures, as the only means of establishing a blood relationship with someone outside of one's immediate consanguineous family. It is a true joining in blood, through a solemn exchange of promises, of two beings who were not previously related. And in this way it bears an uncanny correspondence to the new relationship that comes about between man and God through the promises of faith sealed by the blood of Christ. For by bleeding for us, God in His Son Jesus solemnly joined Himself to humanity, enabling Christians to become His own blood relatives and thus inheritors of His kingdom. Nothing, therefore, is stronger than blood and covenant, for these have been the Lord's own means for bringing the human race into relationship with Himself.

That is why Jesus is not simply the founder or head of the Church, but its husband. For the profound personal bond between a husband and wife on earth has no parallel in interpersonal depth except in the relationship a Christian believer has with his Savior Jesus, which also, mystically, is a bond of marriage. Earthly marriage provides us with a practical picture or working example, then, of what it means to submit to a personal God, what it means to invite the real historical person Jesus Christ to be our Lord and to interfere permanently in our lives. For our God is not a code of moral laws or a theocratic system or an abstract ideal of love, but a person. It is a person with whom we have to do, and that is the reality Christ came to present to the world. And neither is He just one person, but three, three persons inscrutably united in one being.

This is an overwhelming reality to have to come to grips with, and perhaps it is little wonder if many people seek at any cost to evade it, just as they try to sidestep the deepest challenges of marriage. This sort of religion is repugnant to them for the same reason that they shrink from the hard problems of marriage: It isn't abstract enough. What they fail to realize is that God is not abstract, not in the least. He is Spirit, but He is not abstract, and in fact He is the very opposite of abstract. He is the Lord, the very Creator of reality. And He is every bit as close to and involved with us as is a wife or a husband, only unimaginably more so.

Winning Through Surrender

Naturally there is an important difference between the submission we render to God and the submission we may owe to a fellow human being. For we submit to God just because He is God and

He is perfect. But if we submit to other people, it is precisely because they are not perfect, and so are desperately in need of the humble service of our love. "Be careful," warns Paul, "that the exercise of your freedom does not become a stumbling block to the weak.... Never do anything offensive to anyone" (1 Corinthians 8:9; 10:32). Marriage is the natural place to begin, and to practice daily, the curbing of our own freedoms wherever they prove offensive to the other person. If Mary really cannot stand the noise of the power saw, then is it John's place to question her reasonableness or to make slighting comments about the fairer sex or to point out that her food mixer makes even more noise? Or is it rather simply to refrain, in love, from using the saw when Mary is around? That is really all there is to it. It is a simple, pragmatic question of how much John loves Mary: Does he love her enough to stop annoying her with his saw? Is the fact that his wife's peace is being disturbed a matter of greater importance to him than the completion of a birdhouse? For Mary's part, naturally, she needs to make every effort to adjust to the noise of the saw, knowing that a quite innocent pleasure of her husband's is at stake.

Who wins this battle of wills and whims is not the point; the point is that each tries to surrender as much as possible for the sake of the other so that the love between them may be honored and built up in every way—even at the expense of birdhouses and headaches! We need to learn to see that a simple, harmless hobby such as carpentry (or indeed, anything under the sun) may actually become an instrument of the devil if it is allowed to disrupt the love between two people. This is the gist of Paul's advice to the Corinthians, cited above, concerning the attitude a Christian should take toward his "weaker brother." It is a rule that cannot be applied too vigorously in marriage, for ironically it is often the case that each partner assumes the other to be the weaker brother. But if the other really is weaker, argues Paul, then that is all the more reason not to maintain our own rightness, stubbornly and overbearingly, but rather to surrender for the sake of love. Rightness, whenever it seeks to dominate, becomes wrongness, no matter how right it may be. Would we rather be right than happy?

So we give in to God because He is strong and good, but we give in to others because they are weak and sinful, and in the final analysis there are only three parties we must not give in to, and those three are the world, the flesh, and the devil. But the only way to avoid those pitfalls is to give ourselves instead to the Lord and to others in love. For we must give ourselves to someone. We were made for it. We were made for love, for sweet surrender. Marriage, in this as in so many other ways, was specifically designed to enable us to fulfill our heart's desire, which is to acquiesce graciously in all that we were meant to be and to do.

Much has been made of the fact that Paul's advice to wives is to "submit to your husbands," while his advice to the husbands is to "love your wives" (Ephesians 5:22, 25). Some interpreters have delighted in pointing out the distinction between these two commands and the implications this has for the roles of husband and wife. However, the entire passage is prefaced by the command to "submit to one another" (v. 21), and it is clear from the context that Paul intends these words to be directed first of all to Christians in general, but then to have a special relevance for the married couple. In fact, the point seems to be that the married couple is to set the pattern of mutual love and submission for the whole Christian community. If a man cannot lovingly serve his own wife, after all, or a woman her own husband, whom then can they serve? If they cannot bring happiness to one another, how then can they bring happiness to anyone else? Poor

Christian marriages, marriages in which willfulness rules in place of sacrifice, make a laughingstock of the whole church.

It should be clear that in the context of interpersonal relations these two little words, *love* and *submit*, are for all practical purposes synonymous. Surely that is the underlying assumption of Paul's message, and it turns out to be a very succinct statement of the essence of the gospel: To love is to submit, and to submit is to love. How do we know that God loves us? Because in the person of His own Son He "made Himself nothing, took the very nature of a servant…humbled Himself and became obedient to death, even death on a cross" (Philippians 2:7–8).

RISKING IDENTITY

The reclaiming of submission as the heart of love, and particularly of married or covenant love, is without doubt the single most demanding, dangerous, and important task that Christian couples have before them in the modern age. It is a task that runs completely counter to an enormous weight of worldly thought and rhetoric, to say nothing of contradicting some of our most powerful inner drives. For where the task must begin is with a willingness to abandon the self, in fact to throw over the whole egotistical project of selfhood in favor of identification with others, letting go of the old self for the sake of the brand-new and better thing that can be forged only in the fire of self-abnegating love. What is called for is an abandonment so deep and drastic that what we ourselves perceive to be our identity will almost certainly be lost sight of, set adrift. We must be prepared to enter a no-man's-land, a limbo of self-perception, a state that for any other reason but love would be insanity.

Was this not what the Lord Himself chose to do when He threw away the transcendent, invisible cloak in which He had been wrapped since the beginning of time and became a man—and not only a man, but a tiny baby? He must have entered some limbo of self-identity, a limbo such that all the theologians of twenty centuries have been unable to pin down exactly who or what category of being this Bethlehem baby was, except to say that He was a kind of amphibian, both God and man, in a category all by Himself. So stupendously mystifying and unprecedented was this event that it is difficult to understand how even God could have known who He was at that point. All we can say is that at Bethlehem He took a risk, some unimaginable risk of His own skin for our sakes, that somehow God Himself pushed Himself to the very limits and beyond.

But even greater and more mysterious than the risk of the Incarnation was the risk taken at Calvary, when God the Son died, crying out that His own Father had forsaken Him, and when it looked, for the moment, as if the whole grand gamble had failed. Again, who can say who it was, exactly, who died on that cross? How can God die? Has there ever been a more powerful demonstration of an identity crisis, of a soul (God's own) being torn in two? Was the sheer extremity of God's love for us ever more clear? What is the meaning of the Cross if it is not that Jesus Christ went out on a limb for us, into limbo—that God the Son ventured out of His depth in order to bring salvation to His people? The picture is that of a lifeguard plunging into impossibly deep and turbulent waters in order to save a drowning man, while the latter struggles so violently that he actually pulls down his savior with him.

Can we seriously believe that the Lord of the universe takes risks, that in fact He has risked everything for our sakes? Can we believe that it is really possible for the eternal, all-powerful God to lay His life on the line? We had better believe it, for not only is it the heart of Christianity, but it is the mainspring and secret of all love. "Greater love has no man than this, that he lay down his life for his friends" (John 15:13). We must all diminish in this life, we must all go down into the dust of self-annihilation. But by the grace of God in Christ Jesus, this death, this most terrible of all defeats, is itself transformed into the wellspring of love.

It is not that the death of our identities, in and of itself, has any grand meaning or importance. Such a death may accomplish nothing more than to gain us entrance into a psychiatric ward. No, what is necessary is to die for another. If we go out on a limb, we must do it for someone else. We must get so close to the center of another's soul that we feel the ground slipping out from under us and fear for our sanity. We must come out from our dark, protected corners and go near the edge, consenting to the dizzy, bewildering pull that others are able to exert upon us. For God has not kept Himself immaculately sterilized in some hermetically sealed heaven. He is not a huge ego stubbornly clinging to His distant, invulnerable majesty, refusing to give an inch. No, He became one of us, literally sweating, thirsting, suffering—even to the point of being loaded down with our sins, even to the point of dying.

Of course, not everybody wants a dying God on their hands. We do not really want our Lord to have hair on His body, let alone blood oozing out of His wounds. We do not really want love to be breathing down our necks. We never asked for that. Yet that is the sort of God the Lord is, and the simple truth is that in Jesus Christ this God has drawn far too close to us for comfort, knocking against our heart and leaving a messy broken body on our doorstep. And that is supposed to be the pattern for love. Getting too close for comfort. Identifying wholeheartedly with others, regardless of the messiness, heedless of the risk to our own identity, in order that we might be identified with our Lord Jesus Christ.

LOVE AND LIKENESS

Marriage cannot help being a risking of identity. For we gave our-selves into the hands of someone entirely different from ourselves, someone who in many ways may even be opposite to us, who at the very least is a member of the opposite sex. And then we are called upon to cooperate and share with this opposite person in ways that seem to suggest there is really nothing opposite about the two of us at all. Or if there is, there shouldn't be.

Whatever may be said about opposites attracting, when people marry it is always out of a powerful persuasion that they bear some deep (although not always obvious) similarity to one another. It could hardly be otherwise! If a man and woman spend long enough gazing into one another's eyes, they will reach the curious conclusion that they are looking in the same direction, that they are on the same wavelength. And there will be a sense in which they will be right, and there will be another sense in which they could hardly be more mistaken.

Even if a couple has from the outset a healthy perspective on how dissimilar they may really be, still there will be a quiet confi-dence that marriage itself can even out their differences and draw them together. And the strange thing is, this peculiar hope they have is not at all misplaced, for marriage will, very definitely and very forcibly, begin an inexorable process in which whether they like it or not the two of them will come to grow more and more like one another. Oddly, this will be true whether the marriage is a good one or a bad one, so that whatever the basis for common-ality was to begin with, marriage will build and expand upon that. Are both partners service minded, for example, the one expressing service through a deep caring for individuals, and the other through extensive involvement in the leadership of charitable organizations? Then in marriage the two can only grow more and more service minded, and yet in each case the growth will tend to be in the direction of the other person's strength: The organizational person will come to care more for individuals, while the other will grow increasingly to appreciate the value of corporate service. For inevitably, if the marriage lasts, the two must become more and more like one another.

Naturally this tendency can also operate negatively, so that wherever bad habits persist in one partner they will inevitably tend to rub off on the other, and this will come to pass in any one of a number of insidious ways. A marriage may develop into a continuously smoldering cold war, for example, in which each person, by dint of sheer contrariness, becomes ironically a perfect mirror of the behavior of the other, no matter how opposite in character they may appear to be. Or there may be a *Pax Romana*, in which one personality is so thoroughly and aggressively dominant that the other can respond only with an equally thorough, and equally hostile, submissiveness. Or again, a couple may manage to achieve a highly convincing veneer of affection and cooperation, when in reality what they have achieved is codependency, a conspiracy of sin in which each neurotically nurses and feeds upon the other. Whatever the particular circumstances, these sorts of unions are not marriages of symbiosis but of mutual parasitism.

In any case we human beings were fashioned out of clay, and throughout our lives we continue to be molded. We just cannot resist molding one another and being molded in return. We are mere flesh, mud, soft wax, and the modeling process is an inexorable one. Marriage cannot help but set in motion a relentless program of mutual expropriation of properties, properties that in the beginning neither party had any dream or intention of giving up. It may even be true, as some claim, that old married couples actually come to look alike physically.

So there is a kind of mirror effect operative in marriage, part of which stems from that initial coincidence of wavelengths called "falling in love," but part of which is a growing reality within the demanding structure of marriage itself. As to the former, a couple in love always wills that the love may continue, but as to the latter process, that is something that is almost always resisted. We long, in other words, for the other person (and indeed for the whole world) to be more like ourselves, but we do not wish to be pressed into being like anyone else.

EXISTENCE IS RELATIONSHIP

And so it is that one of the greatest blessings of marriage happens also to be one of its gravest pitfalls, and that is the unavoidable tendency of each partner to regard the other as an aspect of themselves, or even as a sort of second self. This is a perfectly legitimate perspective to have, since marriage does take two separate people and mysteriously unite them in "one flesh," as we have seen. Where this pattern goes awry, however, is in the insidious ambition of each partner to see to it that this new united flesh will have as many of his own characteristics and as few of the other person's as possible. For our natural desire is not to participate in a new flesh at all, but rather to suck other people into our own existing flesh, old and moribund as it is. Secretly what we want is not a mate but a duplicate of ourselves. For the self is like a great sucking vacuum, which though nothing in itself, never thinks of looking outside of itself for fulfillment but instead exerts a powerful drag on everything around it.

There is a sense in which we cannot help being like this,

because our selves are modeled after God's self, whose deepest desire is to transform all other selves into His own likeness. But the Lord is the only one in whom this desire is legitimate, and even He, to show His great love, consented to become one of us, being sucked into the great vacuum of the world and its sin to become quite literally one flesh with us, thus demonstrating that no one need fear becoming what he is not, for love's sake. For if God our Creator took on our flesh, how much more eager we should be to take on His Spirit! And if He who is so far above us was willing to become like us and be our brother, then surely it is a small thing for us to be willing to grow into the likeness of a fellow person, an equal, and thus to embrace solidarity with one another. "Make my joy complete," writes Paul, "by being likeminded, having the same love, being one in spirit and purpose" (Philippians 2:2).

This is the true pattern of what needs to happen in a marriage: each partner growing freely toward the other, unthreatened by the other's virtues and unafraid of the other's vices, and the new entity that is thus created growing together in the likeness of Christ. Of course, this is a far cry from the modern idea of marriage, which sees love as a vehicle for self-fulfillment and talks of the importance of "preserving one's individual identity," "respecting differences," "the freedom to be me," and so on. These are important concepts, but they are also easily twisted into propaganda for selfishness. What they can work out to mean in practice may not be a preservation of that special individuality of each person as created by God but rather the cramming of personhood into the narrow box of ego, as if a person were nothing more than his own self-centered plans for himself, his own conscious urges and desires. But that is exactly what marriage works against, attacking self-centeredness in all its disguises, systematically and tirelessly throwing the ego off balance. Any movement by either of the partners toward individuality (in the modern, corrupt sense of the word) will prove to be treacherous for their love. For in marriage we learn to see individuality not as something to be grasped at and carved out by ourselves but rather as a gift bestowed on us by God and by those who love us, within the living matrix of an intimate relationship. Our identity is not what we take into a relationship but what we draw out of it. It is something we do not have at all unless we discover it through reciprocity with others.

The very concept of *person* refers not to any entity in its own right, detachable and independent, but rather to a state of being that is absolutely contingent, arising out of and thoroughly dependent upon mutuality. We exist not in ourselves but only in relation to God and to others, and this truth holds even for God Himself. For the Lord is not one independent person, but three, a trinity that coexists in perfect unity, all the partners being perfect reflections and expressions of one another. Our God, if you like, *is* a marriage, a family whose members are not the least bit ashamed of being utterly like each other and in total agreement about everything. If just one of them (let us say Jesus) had ever for a moment sought independence from the others in order to "be his own person," then there would certainly be no such thing as Christianity. In fact, we can only presume that the whole universe would have fallen apart.

But someone will object: What about the weak person, struggling under the thumb of a powerful, dominant partner? Is submission the answer here too? The fact is, such weak people are often not weak at all. The real question is: Why do they keep giving away their power? When will they own up to their self-defeating behavior? "No one takes my life from me," said Jesus, "but I lay it down of my own accord" (John 10:18). We must not let anyone or anything rob us of life; rather, when we give ourselves, we must give willingly. We must learn mature love and accept no substitutes.

BEARING ONE ANOTHER'S BURDENS

In the final analysis, perhaps we can see that the journey of marriage asks a very simple question of all those who embark upon it. It asks: Can you love another person enough that you will consent to becoming like them? When God asked this question of Himself, in relation to mankind, His answer was Jesus. When Paul asked the question, he answered, "I have become all things to all men so that by all possible means I might save some" (1 Corinthians 9:22). The real test of our love for others comes when we are so intimately involved with them that we cannot help being drawn into their world and sharing their weakness. "Bear one another's burdens," says Paul, "and so fulfill the law of Christ" (Galatians 6:2).

In marriage we are afforded a small glimpse into what it actually must have meant for our Lord Jesus, the Son of God, really and truly to have borne our sins. For it is certainly true that the loved one with whom we dwell and share our whole life bears the brunt of all of our sufferings, complaints, vices, and griefs to such an extent that it might almost be said that they pass through the same experiences we do. They celebrate with us and participate in our times of joy and serenity, but they also share our pains and sorrows in their own bodies and spirits, and often enough they even absorb the blame (God forgive us!) for what are really our own shortcomings. We accuse them, yes, out of our own sin, for it is where we are weak that we are most blind and most tempted to shift the blame. Thus it can truly be said that our loved ones, while not necessarily committing the same sins as we ourselves commit, nevertheless come to partake of the sorrowful results of our sinfulness simply by virtue of their love for us. The more they love, the more they will be burdened by our sin. Love does not shrink from this burden, but willingly shoulders it.

In short, the person we love is inevitably a cross, as well as being a helper in the carrying of our own cross. Why must this be so? Simply because it is impossible to love anyone without seeing intimately into the tragedy of that life. To love is not just to view someone as the most wonderful person in the world or as some kind of saint. It is also to see all the weakness, the falseness and shoddiness, all the very worst in the loved one exposed—and then to be enabled, by the pure grace of God, not only to accept this person, but to accept in a deeper, more perfect way than was possible before. Love works for two people, in other words, the way faith works for one. For faith always begins with a frank recognition of one's own sinfulness (called repentance), which paradoxically opens up the way for greater self-acceptance through forgiveness. Similarly, before love can really begin to be love, it must face and forgive the very worst in the person loved.

In marriage, a wife's imperfections are not something a husband can afford to hold against her, but neither can he afford simply to overlook them. Rather he must bear them with her as part of his cross, just as she bears with him. To live with her in love is to experience at close quarters the way she herself struggles with her own humanness. Is such intimate and costly knowledge to be repaid with criticism? No, it can be answered only with tenderness and compassion and borne with a profound sadness that in turn makes room for more and more love. In this way, love not only falls from heaven but rises from the earth. To love is to be caught in the vortex of another's humanity, to spiral down and down into the murky, tragic tangles of the sinful flesh, where only pure love can go without being defiled. If hatred often consists in being repelled by mere impressions, by surface characteristics in other people who happen to rub us the wrong way, then love consists in seeing into the very center of the twistedness and sin and self-love that are in the heart of another person and yet not being repelled: holding on to the grace by which we ourselves are loved and finding in it the strength to descend with another into their darkest place. If we love other people for their saintliness, then we do not love at all. Love is wasted on saints. It is meant for the sinner.

When we really come to understand and accept this in our own personal love relationships (and there is no better place to see it than in a marriage), it becomes easier for us to grasp the theological doctrine of the atonement. It is easier to comprehend how the Lord, who is so much closer than any human lover, closer to us even than we are to ourselves, has actually taken it upon Himself to stand in our place and to bear not only the consequences but the full blame for all of our sins. Not that our sin is in any way at all God's fault—but nevertheless He has assumed all responsibility for it. That is not the popular way of showing love, but that is God's way. In Jesus He has demonstrated the fullest extremity of this sin-bearing, self-immolating love.

Perhaps it is not hard to see, either, that this is an entirely lost cause, a hopeless waste of effort on the part of our Lord, unless we devote ourselves entirely to Jesus in return. It would be as pointless as if we ourselves were to try to bear the burdens of some long-lost high school sweetheart who had jilted and rejected us and never been heard from again. The Lord bears the sins of all equally, of course, but it does those little good who refuse the offer of His loving mercy. Perfect love is still perfect even when it is one-sided, but the place where it shines most brightly and performs the job that it was intended to do is in a covenant relationship—such as the

Lord has with His people, such as a man has with his wife. Here it is that "love covers a multitude of sins."

PERFECT FOR ONE ANOTHER

Finally, perhaps we can see that Christian submission finds its truest expression not in taking orders or obeying rules or going along with others' whims, nor even in bearing patiently others' weaknesses. Those are all concepts the whole world is familiar with. To the Christian, however, submission means much more: It means a willing involvement in another's sin. It does not mean complicity with sin, but it does imply a sharing of its cost, its wages. A Christian finds the strength to forgive another person, first of all in the fact of his own forgiveness, but secondly in the knowledge that he himself is being crushed by the other's sin. He must forgive, in short, or be destroyed himself. True submission is humility acquired on behalf of another.

When this truth is allowed to operate within a marriage, a miracle takes place. What happens, in essence, is that the partners no longer have any reason to fear one another, for where each becomes willing to bear the other's punishment, the true root of fear has disintegrated. "Perfect love drives out fear, because fear has to do with punishment" (1 John 4:18). It goes without saying that we will cooperate with one another, be obedient, bear faults patiently—yet not because of the teeth-gritting exercise of some abstract virtue but rather because we are no longer afraid of the other's failings, no longer afraid that another's style will cramp ours or drag us down. We are not personally threatened by anger or pride or stubbornness in our mate, any more than by a physical sickness. We are not threatened, in fact, by the other's sin, for we have already come to terms with the worst of it, and already we have forgiven, just as we ourselves have been forgiven. And, therefore, we are able to see one another as God Himself sees us: pure, spotless, perfect.

It is not that we are fooled into thinking that our partner is a perfect person or a perfected Christian, or is in any sense perfect in themselves. Rather, it is simply that we become willing to see this person as a perfect wife or husband, even as *the* perfect wife or husband: that is, the perfect one *for us*, the very one we need. For there is, strictly speaking, no such thing as the perfection of individuals, but only of persons within their roles, so that virtue can never claim to be anyone's private trophy or achievement, but is always, by very definition, shared. The only real perfection that exists is what may be called *relational* (as opposed to *functional*) perfection, and while it is understood that in this world none of us will ever be perfect in any absolute sense, it is also understood, and must be taken on faith, that the Lord has already made us perfect in and through the miracle of relationship. We are perfect not by ourselves, but for one another, even as Christ is perfect not on His own but only in His role as the Son, of Man and of God, who "even though He was the Son, learned obedience through suffering, and was made perfect" (Hebrews 5:8–9). He became perfect, in other words, through the most extreme submission, and thereby became fully qualified to be His people's loving Savior in their direst need.

Are we too, as husbands and wives, prepared to become fully qualified to be our loved one's helper in every extremity of need?

SEVEN

happy are those who mourn

"Son of man, can these bones live again?"

"Thou knowest, Lord."

—Ezekiel 37:3

Death

THE DEVIL'S MIRACLE

Life is a process of aging, and aging is the steady progress of death within us. Every moment we are alive, we are aging. Every moment of life marks a deeper involvement with death. Life and death are thus intimately connected in our bodies, working side by side, hand in hand. And the right hand knows perfectly well what the left hand is doing. It is no secret, and never has been. Many things have been hidden from the minds of men, but it has always been made entirely clear to them that they are going to die. The day is coming when all our earthly possessions will be swept away, and our very flesh will be required of us. The earth will close over our skin, and it will be like a brown, crumbling leaf that blows away and vanishes.

As plain as this fact is, it is so strange that there are still many throughout the ages who have not believed or accepted it. It requires, oddly enough, a certain degree of faith. For death is a sort of miracle. A miracle, if you like, worked by the devil. For many of us, the most awesome event we will ever witness is the extraction of life before our very eyes from the dear body of a loved one.

It is almost too prodigious a thing to be believed. It cannot be taken in. And yet, it must be believed, must be grasped. For as abstract and incredible, conceptually, as death may seem, it is still indisputably the most concrete of all realities. Philosophers speculate on the existence or nonexistence of tables, but there is no argument about the existence of death. All the evidence of our senses points to it, even though an enormous weight of another kind of evidence (the kind of evidence that does not stand up in courts or laboratories) cries out against it.

Death is something that, like odds or like suspense, builds throughout our life. It builds by slow degrees of awareness like the unfolding of a murder mystery in which we ourselves turn out to be the victim. The tension of death mounts in our very cells until, in a way, it explodes inside of us, spewing every one of our precious atoms back to wherever it was they all came from.

The Black Velvet Curtain

For all of us who survive into adulthood, then, there comes a time when we must realize not only that we do not have the world by the tail anymore, but that very possibly the world as we know it is not even on our side. We may decide that the world is actually our enemy, fundamentally antagonistic to our deepest drives and ambitions: to be secure, to be successful, to live forever, to be loved. If our first conscious view of the world, as children, was as a playground—as a place in which everything was provided for us and where our only job was to play all day long—then it is not too hard to comprehend our disappointment in discovering that in some ways this was all a carefully constructed illusion, that perhaps the world is not a playground at all but more a sort of concentration camp: a place in which we must make our way by the sweat of our brows, and where eventually we must die. There is no escaping over the barbed wire.

This is the point at which death becomes a conscious reality to us. For real feelings about it, such as fear and disgust and bitter resentment, have begun to set in, and death is no more a surprise tragic ending to an otherwise-happy tale but something we must face every day, something that looms larger and larger in our hearts as we grow older and are drawn inexorably into its weird circle. As children, we stood shyly in a group on the playground and hoped we would soon be picked for one of the two teams that were forming up. Now it may appear that there is only one team, and we dearly hope that somehow we may escape being picked for it. At least, we do not wish to be picked today. Any day but today.

And so we die not once, but a little every day. Death eats away at our lives, sometimes quite literally, but more often content just casually to knock out one prop after another from under us, until one day we find ourselves with a rope around our necks and nothing beneath our feet but a vast abyss.

This is the backdrop against which millions of lives are lived out: not a backdrop of beautiful scenery, or of anything at all, but one of black, empty space. Lives are curlicues of fire cut briefly in the dark with a glowing stick. This is the earth we have walked on, this the simple basic background that has made possible all of our complexity. Death is the black velvet curtain against which human beings play out all the drama not only of their lives, but of their loves. Love, indeed, is thought universally to be the brightest comet trail of all in this dark heaven, the fire at the very center of life, a fire brighter almost than that of life itself. Even atheists may place faith in love, and it is probably no accident if the point at which we wake up to the reality of death corresponds with the time when we begin to become capable of mature love.

It is almost as if love were a sort of response to death, even a pact against it.

This has always been a well-known phenomenon: that love, like the very best of gourmet sauces, brings out the flavor of death. There are other things that floodlight death, but none that give it such poignancy. This is excruciatingly true of romantic love, but it is much, much truer of married love. There is a way in which marriage and death are themselves a pair of lovers.

BURIED INTO ONE ANOTHER

There is something about putting your mouth on another human mouth, entwining fingers, embracing, exchanging vows of love, and living day in and day out in the presence of another person, that is at once a denial and an affirmation of death. There is something radically insurrectionist about it, yet also something acquiescent. There is a sense of the two of you alone together on a windswept alien planet, clinging to one another for warmth; but there is also the sense of an invincible alliance, the bold formation of something that is ultimately stronger than anything the enemy can throw at you.

A man, on the eve of his wedding day, knows this perfectly well. He knows that something in his manhood is going down to a bitter and ignominious defeat. Nonetheless he is joyful and defiantly confident. Trembling in his boots and wracked by doubts, still he is jubilant and certain. He goes forward like a man to the gas chamber, yet somehow the happiest fellow on earth. Death doesn't matter when you're in love—and yet, neither has it ever been more to the point.

A wedding might even be thought of as the opposite of a funeral: Instead of one person being buried in the earth, two people are buried into one another. In any case death will continue to haunt a marriage, even though (or precisely because) love is a conspiracy against it. And this is true, strangely enough, whether the marriage is such a good one that any separation would be unthinkable, or whether in fact the marriage is so troubled that each partner longs secretly for the other's death.

Whatever the situation, death hovers over a marriage in a way even more extraordinary than it does over an individual life, with almost double the potential impact. Death looms in front of marriage like a gigantic face appearing in a window at night, and in a certain very primal way marriage may almost be understood as a charm against this apparition. This is nowhere more apparent than in that most natural yet overwhelming of drives that is present in all marriages—the drive to produce children. For to many people a child, carefully nurtured and protected, is the human race's only satisfactory means of hurling an insult at death and perhaps even getting the better of it.

Yet if it is true that marriage intensifies the darkness of death's shadow, then surely having a child makes it darker still. The threat, the risk, the potential for tragedy are all tripled when shared three ways. Death becomes a more fearsome foe in a family than it is in a single life, for an individual dies once, while a family may be visited many times by death. And what is more devastating or incomprehensible than the death of a child? And is not the loss of a loved child felt as a much greater tragedy than the death of an orphan? A family knows all of this instinctively, and that is why there is no individual, no unit, no other organization on earth that is more protective of human life, and so more agonized by death, than is the family.

All in all, it is impossible to say whether the ultimate effect of marriage or of children or of love itself is actually to hold death at bay outside the charmed, glowing circle of shared life, or rather to bring death overwhelmingly nearer. It is true that the very existence of death gives love an urgency, a poignancy, and even a clarity that might not otherwise be there. But surely the opposite is true as well: that life without love would render death less odious. The capacity to love, in fact, may be understood in part as a God-given wisdom or clarity of vision that enables us to perceive more fully the horror of death and thereby to feel more acutely its sting.

For to loathe death is really to loathe its sting, which is sin; and sin, in turn, is separation from God; so that when people fear and despise death (and this is true even of people who do not know God), what they really despise—if only they could know it!—is the thought of separation from Him.

RESURRECTION

In a marriage, there is really nothing to do about this gruesome, unwelcome visitor in black—this heightened sensitivity to death—except to allow him to come in, even deliberately to involve and include him in the most mundane affairs of daily life, and then to make use of his presence as an opportunity to lift one's thoughts to God. *Memento mori* must be translated into *memento Dei*. Marriage, in fact, turns out to be a most proper and conducive setting for the religious contemplation of death, leading into the contemplation of eternity and of the Lord Himself.

If the mere existence of death seems to have the effect of enriching love, then why not use it that way? Is not our love for a dear one at its deepest and most intense at the very point of the loved one's death? Is there anything that more increases the sheer value of another person in our eyes than to see them at death's doorstep and to know that in only a little while they will be gone from the face of the earth? Why not strive to live each day not only as if it were our last, or even the last for the whole world, but the last for some one particular person whom we love? For indeed, it may well be. Then, far from being a black cloud hanging over our love, constantly threatening deluge, the presence of death may be converted into a spring, watering our thoughts with the preciousness of life and of each moment, and with the cherishing of our hope in eternity through the resurrection of our Lord Jesus Christ.

When I hold my wife's head in my lap, therefore, and move my hands over the warm, taut, smooth, amazing skin of her face and through the feathered corn silk wonder of her hair, I like to think about the skull underneath. I like to think also about the rushing of her blood through its intricate network of arteries, about the unbelievable meshing of muscles and nerve fibers, about the soft, intestinal coils of her brain, and the fantastic flashing switchboard panels in there and the firings across synapses and all the interior workings of every one of her life-swollen cells. I like to wonder about how in the world all the infinite delicacy of my wife's facial expressions can emerge from these millions of little flesh-and-blood factories, like water from a rock. I like just to drink in the whole breathtaking artistry of physics and biophysics and metaphysics and quantum mechanics and extraterrestrial chemistry and divine grace that have gone into the making of her.

But I like also to think about her skull. I like to ponder its white, delicate porcelain, and that strange, hollow stare it has as it peers wide-eyed and drop-jawed into the ends of time. I find this thrilling—every bit as thrilling, at times, as the curve and thrust of her breasts. Death has its own eroticism, for the nerve center of the erotic lies not in the sexual organs, but in mortality itself.

I don't think there is anything in the least morbid about this. The skull is there, after all; is there any special virtue in pretending it isn't? The fact that it is there at all, indeed, and that human bones so mockingly outlast their proprietors, is something of a cosmic irony, an enigma so deep yet so meticulously and conspicuously *planned*, that surely it must have been set up deliberately (it seems to me) to stimulate contemplation, to tease us out of thought—and into prayer. For in this very puzzle—that the hard, white, staring bones are covered with living, beautiful, glowing flesh that in time is doomed to shrivel up and fall away like an old husk from a kernel—right here lies the ground into which the seed of faith must fall. A thousand questions bump their heads on this low ceiling: why such staggering beauty? and why so brief? why anything at all, instead of nothing? why live if only to die? It is not the salvation of our souls we mortals are primarily worried about, but the salvation of our poor, dear bodies. It is our precious hides from which we cannot imagine being parted.

Yet as I explore with the flesh-coated tips of my own bony fingers around the rims of my wife's eye sockets, what astounds me is that there should have been anything there in the first place, anything in those holes at all, let alone the beautiful, gleaming, personalized jelly of my wife's brown eyes. They mean so much more to me simply because they ought not to be there. They are not such miracles until I view them as they really are, floating impossibly in the dark grottoes of the skull, suspended like the earth itself in cavernous space.

I need this skull; I need its terrible and maddeningly erotic question mark: Life is more here, more round and warm and voluptuous for being placed so lovingly on this black velvet cushion, for being perched on the edge of an abyss.

Ezekiel knew this, and that is why he prophesied the mystery of God's redeeming love from a valley of dry bones. The Lord picked him up and set him down in the middle of the scrap heap of Death's banquet, in the very boneyard of the human race, making him "walk up and down among the vast quantities of bones the whole length of the valley" (Ezekiel 37:2), forcing him to look Death square in its empty, bone-rimmed eye, and to consider long and hard what a human being consists of when stripped of its breath and its warm, vibrant coat of flesh. As Hamlet, the first existentialist in Western literature, looked at the skull of Yorick in a Danish churchyard, he reflected that the final destiny of a man's life might be to be reduced to a wad of clay suitable for stopping a bunghole. But what Ezekiel sees, in the very dryness and deadness of bleached bones, is the miracle of the Lord God's gracious love in ever having breathed life into them in the first place and His amazing promise to call His faithful ones even out of their graves. For what the Lord has done once, can He not do once more?

"Son of man, can these bones live again?—Thou knowest, Lord."

EULOGY

And so we learn that the best married love, from beginning to end, must borrow something from the atmosphere of the victorious Christian funeral. There is always a band of ironic, mournfully jubilant New Orleans minstrels winding its way through the hearts of those who really love. For they, even more than others, are called to a daily mourning over one another, a daily anointing and preparation for death. That is how Mary showed her love for Jesus, pouring costly ointment on His living flesh, scandalously preparing His healthy body for burial (John 12:3). Yet how many have died without any such homage, leaving behind huge, gaping wounds of unbearable regret in the hearts of those who said they loved them: regret for not having loved them in life as they discover, so painfully, they do in death?

Somehow we must learn to mourn our loved while they are yet alive, not waiting until they are gone and our grief does no one but ourselves any good. At least one kiss each day should be watered with tears and planted on bone. For this sort of wake is really wonder, devotion, faith—wakefulness indeed! The bones must be acknowledged, our respects paid, before the flesh can be celebrated, and love must grapple in advance with remorse, drawing out its sting with little daily acts of tribute. For now is the time to eulogize, now the time to deck with flowers. Today is the day to carry to its rest the whole weight of our love's flesh upon our shoulders.

EIGHT

in the winepress

Oneness

"They are no longer two, but one."

—Matthew 19:6

❧ Oneness ❧

Do You Love Her?

This book could easily have been titled *A Funny Thing Happened on the Way to the Monastery.* It's the thoughts of a would-be monk who stumbled into marriage and discovered, in the exquisite, excruciating winepress of conjugal love, that no spirituality is more profound, no Christian discipline more exacting, no monastic life more fulfilling than the loving arms of a wife.

At a time when I thought I'd given up on women forever, I met Karen and fell in love. Confused, panicked, desperate, I sought the counsel of a Jesuit priest I'd studied classical literature with in university. I felt sure that as a celibate himself, he'd give me the advice I sought: "Flee temptation, my son, and get thee to a monastery!" Instead this wise, kindly old man, peering at me mistily over his glasses, asked me one simple question: "Do you love her?"

I should have known right then that I was caught. But stubborn dolt that I was, I failed to see the point. Not that the question was difficult. Oh no! I was able to answer without hesitation. To my own shame, I quote verbatim my response: "Of course I love her. But what does that have to do with it?"

How could I not have known that love has *everything* to do with it? For the Christian, especially, love rules. Love is king, for the King Himself is love. Through a gift of love God had already directed me. How often does it happen in the Christian life that God has already led, already shone the light, while frantically we seek His counsel? This is because we're afraid to follow. We're afraid of love, because we know that to be love's disciple is to abandon all else.

So, armed with obtuse trepidation, back I went to Karen and told her we had to break up. She cried, I relented, and six months later we were married.

Did marriage resolve my desperate dilemma? No. It took probably two more years of doubts, misgivings, second guesses, and cold sweats before I finally threw in the towel and accepted that I was good and thoroughly married and there'd be no running off to any monastery for me. I'd made my bed—or rather, Karen and I and the Lord together had made it—and now it was time to lie down in peace. Which I've done, mostly, ever since.

This book, however, did not emerge from the peaceful resolution of my conflict, but rather from the midst of the fire. As noted in the preface, most of my ideas were written down during the tumultuous period of our engagement and assembled into a book a year or so later. If I was going to be married, I had to have a good reason for it, a rationale. I already had a theology for celibacy; now I needed a theology for marriage. This didn't come easily; I had to hammer it out. I wanted to live a heroic life and I didn't think heroes got married. God changed my mind. He converted me from viewing marriage as a trap to embracing it as a high and holy calling. In the process I learned that this is precisely the path of Christian discipleship—coming to understand that the ordinary way is really the glorious way, the lowly is really the lofty.

ONENESS IN SPIRIT

Plainly, this book did not grow out of years of experience or out of any great wisdom, but rather just the opposite. How can this be? At times of crisis, I believe, the Lord may give us a blueprint—a plan not just for navigating the crisis but for all that lies ahead. Receiving the blueprint is not the same as being wise; wisdom comes only with building the house, with actually living out what has been shown in vision. Thus great books can be written by fools.

In the twenty years since my book was first published, many readers, knowing its humble origins, have asked whether I might now make any changes or additions in the light of practical experience. My answer to this, until recently, was always no. The original blueprint has proven amazingly accurate and, by following it, our house has risen on a firm foundation into a palace of joy.

However, for this twentieth anniversary edition of *The Mystery of Marriage,* there is one new thought I'd like to explore. A first glimmer of this came to me when we'd been married for about ten years. I was working in my study one day when a knock came on the door. I opened to a stranger who introduced himself as a fan of my book who wondered if he might have a word with me.

After describing some of the ways he and his wife had been blessed by my writing, this man gave me a searching look and said, "Just one thing is missing from your book, and I'm surprised you didn't address it."

"Oh? What's that?" I was all ears.

"Oneness. Why didn't you write about *oneness in spirit?"*

I was stunned. There was an obviousness to this comment, yet also a profundity that I could not plumb. It's as if someone had just acquainted me with the facts of life—the staggering notion that a couple could have a baby! I had to admit to this man that I had not written about oneness in spirit because I had not experienced it. Of course, that hadn't stopped me from writing about many other matters I knew little of, and in rereading my book now, I see that it does contain a good many hints of oneness. However, the topic is never tackled head-on.

For a long time after the encounter with this visitor I pondered the strange idea of oneness, and for a long time that's all it was—an idea. Yet more and more it struck me as, of all the mysteries of marriage, the deepest and most beautiful. At the same time I knew (or thought I knew) that Karen and I did not have oneness in our marriage.

I say "*thought* I knew" because, in fact, we did have oneness, and had had it all along. From the moment we exchanged rings and vows at the altar, the Lord had made us one. This is what marriage is; the very word means a *joining* or *uniting*. As Jesus taught, "They are no longer two, but one. Therefore what God has joined together, let man not separate" (Matthew 19:6).

So Karen and I had been one all along. We just didn't feel it. Herein lies another way in which marriage reflects our relationship with God. From the moment a person first believes in Christ he is united to God in spirit, yet it's the work of a lifetime to fully realize this oneness in daily life. How important is this realization? All-important. I venture to say that the whole of the Christian life rests upon the reality of our oneness with Christ. As Paul put it, "I have been crucified with Christ and I no longer live, but Christ lives in me" (Galatians 2:20). To become a Christian is to do away with one self so that another—a new self united to Christ—is resurrected in its place. This resurrection, or new life, is made possible precisely because of the phenomenon of union.

Is union with God a mountain to be climbed, a reward for

extravagant effort? Is divine union reserved for the greatest of saints and mystics? Not at all. Union is for everyone, for every Christian, from the greatest to the least. Again, does union with God take place gradually over many years as a Christian matures through countless experiences? No, it takes place once and for all at the moment of conversion, as surely as a new life is conceived at the union of egg and sperm. Yes, the new soul in Christ has much growing to do. Yet growth does not happen apart from Christ (how could it?) but in union with Him. Everything depends upon the fact that, through Jesus, we're directly connected to God.

I stress this point because all progress in spirituality comes, not from striving to be closer to God, but rather from realizing and accepting that already we're one with Him. Already Christ lives in us by faith. Already we've been reconciled to God through the blood of Jesus that, like a red carpet, has been rolled out in our souls so that we, the honored guests of heaven, may approach the highest throne with full confidence.

A State of Realization

How are we to respond to the astounding news of our oneness with God? By groveling in the dust for some way to please Him? No, that is not how faith is arrived at in the first place, nor is it how faith grows. This is why Scripture keeps telling us, "Peace!… Don't worry…. Don't be afraid." Our God is already with us and in us and wants us to rest in His arms, full of thanks and wonder, basking in relief and joy. In this state, the path of life opens up. Do we want to hear God, know Him, follow Him? This is the way. We begin at the very point where we assume we must end. We begin in heaven, not on earth. For already God has "raised us up with

Christ and seated us with him in the heavenly realms in Christ Jesus" (Ephesians 2:6).

Surprisingly, this same topsy-turvy wisdom applies to marriage. We've already given our life to the other person, already rolled out the red carpet. The look of love, after which nothing is ever the same again, has already passed between us. The words and the rings have already been exchanged, the knot already tied. There's no going back. Yet neither need we move an inch in order to advance. It's all a matter of realizing what has already taken place. What began with a look is continually refreshed, simply with a look.

The early days of love and courtship are all realization, all an entranced basking in the blazing light of the free gift of love so astoundingly bestowed. But what about later, when the glorious gift lies buried beneath the mundanity and stress of married life? Then the state of realization must be recovered, pure and simple. No progress can be made without the recovery of the original miracle. The unity of love cannot be forged anew, for it was never forged in the first place. It was given. Suddenly it was *there*, and it hasn't gone anywhere. It is still, always has been, just there. Realize it, be thankful, and live in the joy of oneness.

What strange advice this is—that to be at peace with our spouse, we should simply be at peace. Yet this is all the advice the Bible offers. Over and over we hear, "Be at peace with each other.... Don't quarrel.... Get rid of anger." If only we could grasp who it is we're yelling at, picking at, berating, manipulating. If only we could remember who lies in the bed beside us or looks back at us across the breakfast table. It is (or might as well be) ourselves! Paul says exactly this in Ephesians 5:28–29: "He who loves his wife loves himself. After all, no one ever hated his own body, but he feeds and cares for it."

The Old Testament prophet Malachi says the same. Do you wonder why God isn't paying attention to you? "It is because the LORD is acting as the witness between you and the wife of your youth, because you have broken faith with her, though she is your partner, the wife of your marriage covenant. Has not the LORD made them one? In flesh and spirit they are his" (2:14–15).

What keeps a marriage healthy, what keeps a Christian life healthy, what the Bible keeps trying to tell us, is that everything comes down to a realization, a recognition, of the truth. A husband and wife are one, as Christ and the spirit are one. Will we live as one, or seek to go our own way?

HYPOSTASIS

At the beginning of creation "God saw all that he had made, and it was very good" (Genesis 1:31). But He also saw one thing that wasn't good. We read about the one problem in Genesis 2:18, where the Lord says, "It is not good for the man to be alone."

These words follow immediately upon His warning to Adam not to eat from the tree of knowledge, "for when you eat of it you will surely die." Apparently God knew that Adam, left to himself, would be less able to resist temptation. The Lord identified a potential weakness in His creation—or at least an incompleteness—and the answer to this was Eve. Eve was created (and with her, the order of marriage) to make humanity and all of creation strong and complete. To complain that Eve also made humanity more vulnerable (for did she not yield to temptation first?) is to overlook the greater truth that one of her kind—without any help from a man—bore the Savior of the world.

Through vulnerability comes strength, for God's "power is made perfect in weakness" (2 Corinthians 12:9). Marriage, paradoxically, makes people stronger by making them more vulnerable. Vulnerability allows for intimacy—or as the word is sometimes rendered, *into-me-see*. Marriage exploits the fact that humans are not opaque but are full of holes. Eyes, mouths, ears, sexual orifices are the channels for intimate communion. Through our cracks, love gets in.

A crack was how it all started, when the Lord God "took part of the man's side" and "made a woman from the part he had taken out of the man" (Genesis 2:21–22). Ever since then the man and the woman have been trying to get back together, seeking to recapture their essential oneness. The act of sex, in itself, goes only so far toward this goal. The more perfect solution is marriage.

Ever since God brought the first woman to the first man, this has been His main business in the world—drawing people together into unity. Marriage is a living demonstration of the extravagant intimacy into which God wishes to draw all people, with the intent, as Jesus prays to His Father, "that they may be one as we are one: I in them and you in me. May they be brought to complete unity to let the world know that you sent me and have loved them even as you have loved me" (John 17:22–23).

Consider how remarkably dissimilar are the members of the Trinity: one the majestic Father of all; one a humble man who walked the earth; one a wind, a fire, an inscrutable Spirit. Any one of these divine persons would do very nicely for a God. Why must they boggle the mind by subsisting together in perfect unity? The Greeks had many gods, but they were jealous of each other and fought. The members of the Trinity, by contrast, are so united that, distinct and all-powerful though each is, they are not separate, but one God.

Marriage reflects the mystery of the Godhead by being a true union of persons. There is a word for this dynamic of oneness:

hypostasis. A hypostatic union is one in which distinct identities amalgamate to form one new identity. The verb *hypostatize* means to make into, or regard as, a distinct or personal reality. When Adam delivered his famous wedding speech in Genesis 2:23—"This is now bone of my bones and flesh of my flesh"—he was hypostatizing the relationship between himself and Eve. That is, he was declaring the two of them to be (despite outward appearances) not two, but one. Inspired by the Holy Spirit, he saw himself and his new wife as God saw them—not as two separate individuals but as a union. Two persons, yes; but two persons existing in a hypostatic union. Truly married.

THE EDGE OF A SWORD

What is oneness? Recently I talked to an engaged couple who described their relationship in rapturous tones. "It's as if we're on the same wavelength about everything," they crowed. "We think the same way, have the same way of doing things, share the same vision and dreams. It's amazing!"

This won't last. Marriage is not about sameness, but about oneness, which is characterized less by similarities than by differences. One partner is a man, the other a woman, and that's just the beginning. One is sociable, the other reclusive; one prefers sunshine, the other clouds and rain; one loves poetry, the other scorns it; one is punctual, the other (to put it politely) lives largely free of the constraints of time; one likes a down quilt for sleeping, the other a light blanket. How can two such opposites ever be one? Might as well ask how a glove fits a hand, or how black print appears on a white page. Oneness arises from differences fitting together, from contrasts corresponding.

Naturally Karen and I share much in common. But not that

much. The greatest correspondence is our shared faith, which makes up for a great deal. But even here, there are dramatic differences in the way we think about and practice our faith. The wonder is that we get along at all.

How then do we know we're one? How is oneness manifest? I could tell some dramatic stories. One day while driving in traffic Karen felt a tingling on top of her head—a characteristic sign for her of the Holy Spirit's presence. With the tingling came a sense that, without knowing why, she needed to pray for me. Later, comparing notes, we realized that at the same moment, a hundred miles away, I experienced a tremendous spiritual breakthrough.

Even more telling than such remarkable events, however, are the everyday ones. I'll work all day at my desk with the phone turned off, when suddenly it occurs to me to turn it on, and one minute later Karen calls. Or I'll be watching her prepare supper in the kitchen and I'll know, with sudden piquancy, that right here, with her, is my home. Or we'll be walking together and I'll take her hand, and all at once I'm not just aware of her, but I know she's a part of me. Or we'll be talking or praying, and the words she says are the very words I need to hear, the very ones that fill in the blanks of my own perplexity.

Oneness gives the freedom to speak one's mind to the other about absolutely anything. Oneness is as comfortable with silence as with speech. Oneness inspires perfect trust. Oneness means being the same person away from one's spouse as with him or her. Oneness anticipates the other's needs, and feels the other's hurts as one's own. Oneness willingly sets aside differences for the simple joy of living in peace. Oneness blossoms into a mutually fulfilling sex life. Oneness looks into the eyes of the loved one for a long, long, unbroken time while making love.

A deep awareness of oneness spells the end of fighting. Of course, the very week I've been writing this chapter, Karen and I have (uncharacteristically) locked horns. Oneness in marriage, as with God, is not a skill to be mastered. Rather it's a phenomenon to be marveled at with increasing humility and gratitude.

To live in oneness is to walk on the edge of a sword, yet never to fear of slipping, for the only wound we'll ever suffer is to our pride. "What causes fights and quarrels among you?" asks James. "Don't they come from your desires that battle within you?... 'God opposes the proud but gives grace to the humble.' Submit yourselves, then, to God" (4:1, 6–7).

UNCONDITIONAL LOVE

How, practically, can a couple submit themselves to God and so discover unity with each other? How can oneness be cherished? There are, to my knowledge, two prerequisites. One is shared prayer, and the other is unconditional love.

Almost every day for over twenty years Karen and I have prayed together. We do so because we worship the same God, but also because we go about our faith so differently. Without these times of shared prayer, our two faiths—though founded on the same theology—might soon have little in common. Couples who do not pray are as badly off as those who stop sleeping together. Like lovemaking, prayer requires, in a sense, taking off the clothes, removing the shoes to touch holy ground. Such acts of deep communion, beyond mere communication, carry tremendous power for healing and renewal.

To pray together is to draw water from the same well. The experience of unity arises from many, many prayers spoken and felt together daily over years. There's only one Holy Spirit, and to pray well is to hear Him, sense Him, give voice to His thoughts and moods. When couples do this honestly, how can they help but enter into the place of unity? Each time they go there, the bond of oneness, the very secret of their marriage, is strengthened. Prayer is a means of returning daily to the altar where husband and wife were first joined.

Shared prayer by itself, however, is not enough to nurture oneness. For sadly, this exercise can grow stale and repetitive, and it's possible for one partner to dominate. Accordingly, a second, more vital ingredient is required: unconditional love.

Of course the word *unconditional* is redundant. Love, to be love, must be unconditional. Yet it seems necessary to spell this out—especially in the context of marriage—as so often the poor, miserable thing that goes by the name of love, which we hope will be enough to sustain a marriage, has no hope of sustaining anything because it is not unconditional. It is not the same love God lavishes so freely upon us, accepting us just as we are without judgment or criticism, without even any requirement for change. Yes, the gospel changes us, but not through expectation or coercion. We change, paradoxically, only as we come into the light of unconditional love and experience the astounding freedom to be exactly as we are.

Is this the love we offer to our spouse? It's the only kind that works. As long as we exert pressure on the other, however subtly, to conform to our agenda, the relationship will stay stuck and the beautiful experience of marital oneness remains a chimera.

Natural human inclination is less toward oneness than toward increasing separation. Only unconditional love is a powerful enough elixir to reverse this trend and to keep a marriage fresh and growing. Indeed such love itself initiates growth by always taking the first step—being first to understand, first to soften the heart, first to forget a wrong, first to shoulder blame. This is the model of Christ, who in order to make peace with the world took our punishment upon Himself. All the centuries of law, of God trying to legislate mankind to do His will, came to naught. Only the gospel, which begins by totally banishing all expectation and regulation, frees the heart to become one with God and to live accordingly.

To love unconditionally is to want the other's way as much as our own—or more precisely, to know that ultimately the other's way *is* our own. For isn't it true that what we really want, at heart, is harmony in our marriage? Wouldn't the achievement of this be far better than any of our selfish wants? Stubbornly to pursue our own way at the expense of oneness with our spouse is to play a self-defeating game. Our God is a relational God, which is why He created Adam *and* Eve. The image of God is not only in the man alone but in a relationship. Only through loving, harmonious relationships can God be known, for He exists in such a relationship Himself.

If you aren't feeling one with your spouse, neither are you experiencing harmony and wholeness in your own soul. If you aren't intimate with your spouse, intimacy with God will suffer. How could it not? Indeed the way you feel right now toward your spouse *is* the way you feel toward God. Any shadow in the one relationship will necessarily fall upon the other. This is why the two great commandments go together: Love God utterly, and your neighbor as yourself.

In a difficult marriage this comes as harsh news. Indeed it's the fact of oneness that makes being in a a bad marriage so awful. The only way forward is for each partner to receive God's unconditional love for himself or for herself, daily, and so to live in the amazing freedom of the children of God, released from all worldly obligations—including the warped demands of an unhealthy marriage. As Romans 8:12 puts it, "We have an obligation—but it is not to the flesh." Our sole obligation is to the Spirit who is "life and peace" (8:6). God wants us to love unconditionally because this alone sets us free.

Amidst all the difficulties of a shared life, unconditional love may not always be felt, but it can always be intended. And in the final analysis this is what counts. God sees and values, not our performance, but the intent of the heart.

CHRISTOPHER RAINBOW

How appropriate that our journey in this book began with "Otherness" and now ends with "Oneness." These two poles define the natural arc of a marriage, the journey of a couple's soul. This is the pattern for a married life, and it's the pattern for each day of that life. The most seasoned of couples will have times each day of experiencing one another as "other," and also times—perhaps even the same times—of knowing themselves to be one. And this is good, for both poles are necessary to produce the electricity that keeps a marriage vibrant.

The same holds true of our life in God. He is Other, and we are one with Him, and there is no contradiction, and so it will remain for all eternity. Hallelujah!

Having expressed all I can in discursive prose about the mysterious reality of oneness in marriage, let me conclude now with a story, a parable in which marriage reflects the soul's union with Christ. It's called "Christopher Rainbow":

With Christopher Rainbow and me, right from the start it was one of those stormy romances: on again, off again, on again, off again. So when the news first came out about this new technique for merging two people into one, we simply made up our minds one night, he and I, to throw caution to the winds and give it a try. I guess it just seemed high time for us to take some kind of permanent, irreversible step, and so we thought—well, why not? *Why not go all the way?*

After all, people are always hopping into bed together these days, and it's nothing for couples to shack up. So when this new method of total fusion was discovered, and we began seeing it advertised everywhere, it just seemed the natural thing for Christopher and me to do.

Of course, I realize it strikes many people as shockingly grotesque, the very idea of two separate people being literally melted down into one. But if you stop to think about it, it's really no more peculiar a thing than shaking hands, say, or kissing—to say nothing of lovemaking! I mean, who ever dreamed up such things? However common they may become, the most ordinary gestures of intimacy retain a savor of strangeness. And ultimately, don't they all point in the same direction, toward deeper and deeper union?

Naturally Christopher and I had a big church ceremony, all the details of which I won't go into. But the moment itself, that moment when the two of us stood there hand in hand before the altar and then suddenly, physically, were melded together—how can I describe that? Well, one thing I'll say is that instead of being inside myself, looking out at Christopher, suddenly I felt that *I was inside Christopher, looking out at myself!* One moment I was minding my own business, more or less, and the next moment I was minding business for Christopher Rainbow.

Looking back, I can see that before then, in spite of having a lover and all, really I was still behaving pretty much like my own person: single, autonomous, marching to a private drum. And expecting Christopher just to tag along! It was almost as though I were the only person on earth, lost in my own little dream world. But ever since that mysterious transaction at the altar, like it or not I've found myself living not my own life but Christopher's: doing Christopher's work, thinking Christopher's thoughts, getting used to Christopher's body as being my own body, and trying, however clumsily, to do all things just the way Christopher wants them done. And since there is legally only one living person now in place of two, I even took his full name, first and last, as my own: *Christopher Rainbow*.

My parents, predictably, were outraged. They'd been dead against the thing all along, refusing even to attend the ceremony. But you should have seen them the day Christopher and I walked into their home as one person! I mean, on top of everything else, Christopher has this thick foreign accent, which to my ears sounds adorable, though I know it turns a lot of people off. So even before we got in the door my parents heard my familiar voice all mixed up with that alien voice. And as soon as they laid eyes on the face of their dear daughter pressed shamelessly into the face of this foreigner, and saw my lips moving with his in a kind of perpetual osculation—well, they just freaked out. They had no idea who I was anymore, they said, and merely to look at me, all wrapped up in that man, sent shivers down their spines.

From the way they carried on you'd have thought I'd been lost to them forever! You'd have thought that getting joined together with a strange man was something unutterably disgusting, even perverted, for a decent woman to do. Well, if it had been anyone besides Christopher Rainbow, I'm sure I'd agree with them. But Christopher just happens to be the soul of decency, a paragon of purity and goodness. And how can you argue with true love?

I don't mean to imply that it's all been smooth sailing for Christopher and me. We've had our ups and downs, believe me, and I can't honestly say I don't ever miss myself, the way I used to be. The fact is, I do get frustrated not being able to run my own show. I know it's silly, since there's no going back now. But it's one thing to be one with another person, and it's another thing altogether to act as one. In the beginning, especially, the two of us weren't coordinated at all, and I'm sure that's partly what put my family off. It was as though I and a perfect stranger had thrown a moth-eaten blanket over our heads and were pretending to be a dancing horse. We kept stepping on toes, knocking over lamps, getting in each other's way. And we were constantly having these long, tedious discussions about how to work things out. My feeling was that the only sane way to operate was on a fifty-fifty basis: half the time we'd be me, and the other half we'd be him. What could be fairer than that? But Christopher, being from the Old Country, wouldn't hear of it. He seemed determined not just to share my life but to take it over completely.

So it hasn't always been easy, living in Christopher Rainbow, or having him living in me. He can be so difficult to figure out sometimes, so full of inconsistencies. I mean, first he'll say one thing, and then he'll say something else that sounds exactly the opposite. Or we'll be on our way to the supper table, for example—and I'll be starving!—and suddenly he remembers that he has to make this important phone call, and the next minute we're throwing on our coat and heading out the door to some dire emergency. And right in the middle of that, he's liable to stop and spend some time playing with the neighborhood kids! That's just the kind of man he is. You never quite know what he's going to do next. Yet somehow he expects me to keep up with all of this, and even to read his mind. Because he's doing it all, remember, inside of me, right inside my mind and body. Sometimes all I want is just to get on with a few innocent little plans of my own—like vegging in front of the TV, maybe, or fooling around with some of my old friends, or sleeping in on a Sunday morning. I tell you, it can be mighty painful, always being yanked in two directions at once.

But then, I guess the truth is that I felt much more like a schizophrenic before meeting Christopher Rainbow than after. For somehow, in spite of everything, I have to admit I'm more *myself* now than I've ever been. That's why I can so heartily recommend this new technique of fusing people together, whatever little problems it might create. The better I get to know Christopher on the inside, the more his odd behavior on the outside seems not so crazy or inconsistent, but begins to make sense. You really have to walk around in a person's shoes in order to see things their way.

And talk. It takes a lot of talking. Even now, not a day goes by when the two of us don't have to sit down together and sort out the issue of our union and what it all means. Again and again Christopher has to explain patiently to me that what actually happened, that moment before the altar when I got joined to him, was that I *died* to my old existence, and a brand-new person was formed. Can't I see how preposterous it is, he'll argue, for me to keep on trying to revert to my old independent self, when that self is now nothing but a dead shell? When I don't even have a living body to call my own anymore?

"So what about you?" I'll pout. "It's a two-way street, you know. How come you get off scot-free?"

"Oh, but I don't," he answers softly. "Aren't you forgetting that I died too?"

And at that, the very shadow that crosses his face will steal across mine, and I'll feel my lips begin to tremble just as his do, and in my eyes—which are really *our* eyes—the tears will spring. And then in our heart I'll know that he is right. Then I'll know that fifty-fifty is impossible, and that nothing makes sense anymore but for the two of us to become totally and unconditionally identified, immolated into one another.

today in paradise

Epilogue

❧ Epilogue ❧

The first thing I see, as I open my eyes, is the morning making a
pink glow on the trunks of the three birch trees outside our window. Between two of the trunks hangs the moon, just past full and
sinking in the west, the same pale, chalky pink color as the papery
bark of the birches. Both trees and moon appear almost translucent, as if lit from behind.

But the whole morning is translucent. The air holds light like
a goblet. Even the mountain, that most opaque of God's creations,
glows with an inner light. Filling the south window, its soft browns
and grays and greens blend and shine like colors on water. Light
seeps slowly out of its rocks and woods as if it had been stored
there overnight. Near the summit, like an eye shaded under its
brow, lies one small patch of snow from last year, and out of it
springs a tiny silver waterfall that cascades down the mountainside
as if this great pile of rocks had sprung a leak and its silver blood
were pouring out. The water is yet another translucency, a moving
window, liquid light.

Mountain, waterfall, moon, pink-skinned birches—all these are
staggering realities. They are extraordinary things in themselves,
and they are even more extraordinary for their quality of stained-
glass transparency, their quality of pointing beyond themselves to

the much greater reality that lies behind them, to the One True Light with which they are all imbued, in whose light we see light. Can we view the world as a window (albeit a "darkened glass") from which the face of our Lord looks out at us?

This is the scene I wake up to every morning, here where I live, to the accompaniment of one of those frothing, silver-blue, rushing mountain rivers whose sound fills my ears the way the dawn light fills my eyes. And yet even all this is not all. There is something else. Something more breathtaking than any of these other stupendous and beautiful wonders, and even more radiant with light.

There is a woman in bed beside me. Right this moment I could reach out my hand and touch her, as easily as I touch myself, and as I think about this, it is more staggering than any mountain or moon. It is even more staggering, I think, than if this woman happened instead to be an angel (which, come to think of it, she might well be). Only two factors prevent this situation from being so overpoweringly awesome that my heart would explode just trying to take it in: One is that I have woken up just like this, with this same woman beside me, hundreds of times before; and the other is that millions of other men and women are waking up beside each other, just like this, each and every day all around the world, and have been for thousands of years.

Just so easily are miracles unraveled, disqualified, turned back into the common stuff of everyday life. Just so easily do statistics sprinkle their unmagical dust over all the wondrous beauty of life, transforming the celestial into the commonplace, the impossible into the inescapable. Yet if even the miracle of a man and a woman in love can be stripped of its splendor, covered with dust, buried under ordinariness, then what hope have we men and women of ever surviving the monotony of heaven, where love will be as common as air? How shall we cope in an afterlife where there will be nothing miraculous to lift us out of our tedium, because there will be nothing unmiraculous? Here and now, it seems, is the time to practice amazement, the time to learn how to be thunderstruck. Either we suffocate under all that is unbeautiful, unsurprising, unspectacular, ungraceful in our lives, or else we learn here and now to breathe the air of grace. In marriage, to put this thought into more homely language, we learn how to appreciate one another, to see one another as precious. We learn how to love.

And so, practicing already for heaven, it is with an expectancy of grace that I look over in the awakening light of this brand-new day at the woman lying next to me, breathing lightly, like an organ of my own body. She is more beautiful to me than the light itself, more present than this towering mountain, her form under the covers is more elementary than any horizon, and she is closer to me than the air I breathe. She is "bone of my bones, and flesh of my flesh." There are other people in my life, but no one like her. More than anyone else on earth, more even than my own self, she represents the vessel I must and will be poured into. She will have all the very best, the cream, of my love.

She is as close as anyone in the world can come to being for me, in that mournful, radiant flesh of hers, what Christ is to me in the spirit.

The Lover's Hermitage

Love, you are my hermitage,
my dwelling for ever.

Just as a happy bachelor
may aspire to be a hermit,
so as your husband do I dream
of being more married.

Your body is a path leading
through a golden wood;
your love is a clearing
in the center of the forest.

Here have I built my home,
here in you alone.
With you I know a solitude
deeper than my own.

One table, one rocking chair
by the hearth of you—
and in your face a window
brighter than the sky!

Your words are quieter
than my thoughts.
Gladly shall I spend my life
in the cool still hush of you.

When you smile I'm warmed
like earth in the sun.
Your laugh is the brook
at my doorstep.

Gentler are you than breath,
stranger than death.
Just to touch your hair
is more peaceful than sleep.

Surely all my wandering
finds its end in you.
In your brown eyes
may I safely die.

Love, you are my hermitage,
my dwelling for ever.